The Small Museum Toolkit,
Book 1

About the Series

The American Association for State and Local History Book Series publishes technical and professional information for those who practice and support history, and addresses issues critical to the field of state and local history. To submit a proposal or manuscript to the series, please request proposal guidelines from AASLH headquarters: AASLH Book Series, 1717 Church St., Nashville, Tennessee 37203. Telephone: (615) 320-3203. Fax: (615) 327-9013. Website: www.aaslh.org.

About the Organization

The American Association for State and Local History (AASLH), a national history organization headquartered in Nashville, TN, provides leadership, service, and support for its members, who preserve and interpret state and local history in order to make the past more meaningful in American society. AASLH is a membership association representing history organizations and the professionals who work in them. AASLH members are leaders in preserving, researching, and interpreting traces of the American past to connect the people, thoughts, and events of yesterday with the creative memories and abiding concerns of people, communities, and our nation today. In addition to sponsorship of this book series, the Association publishes the periodical *History News*, a newsletter, technical leaflets and reports, and other materials; confers prizes and awards in recognition of outstanding achievement in the field; and supports a broad education program and other activities designed to help members work more effectively. To join the organization, go to www.aaslh.org or contact Membership Services, AASLH, 1717 Church St., Nashville, TN 37203.

The Small Museum Toolkit, Book 1

Leadership, Mission, and Governance

Edited by
Cinnamon Catlin-Legutko
and Stacy Klingler

ALTAMIRA
PRESS

A division of
ROWMAN & LITTLEFIELD PUBLISHERS, INC.
Lanham • New York • Toronto • Plymouth, UK

Published by AltaMira Press
A division of Rowman & Littlefield Publishers, Inc.
A wholly owned subsidiary of The Rowman & Littlefield Publishing Group, Inc.
4501 Forbes Boulevard, Suite 200, Lanham, Maryland 20706
http://www.altamirapress.com

Estover Road, Plymouth PL6 7PY, United Kingdom

British Library Cataloguing in Publication Information Available

Library of Congress Cataloging-in-Publication Data

The small museum toolkit. Book 1, Leadership, mission, and governance / edited by
Cinnamon Catlin-Legutko and Stacy Klingler.
    p. cm. — (American Association for State and Local History book series)
Includes bibliographical references and index.
    ISBN 978-0-7591-1948-2 (cloth : alk. paper) — ISBN 978-0-7591-1335-0 (pbk.
) — ISBN 978-0-7591-1342-8 (electronic)
    1. Small museums—Administration. 2. Small museums—Management. I. Catlin-
Legutko, Cinnamon. II. Klingler, Stacy, 1976– III. Title: Leadership, mission, and
governance.
  AM121.S63 2012
  069.068—dc23   2011028157

Printed in the United States of America

CONTENTS

EDITORS' NOTE

Small museums are faced with the enormous task of matching the responsibilities of a large museum—planning strategically, securing and managing human and financial resources, providing stewardship of collections (including historic buildings) as well as excellent exhibitions, programs, and publications, and responding to changing community and visitor needs—all with more limited human and financial resources. Small museum staff (paid or unpaid) often fulfill key responsibilities outside their area of expertise or training.

We recognize that small museum staff lack time more than anything. To help you in the trenches, we offer this quick reference, written with your working environment in mind, to make the process of becoming a sustainable, valued institution less overwhelming.

The Small Museum Toolkit is designed as a single collection of short, readable books that provides the starting point for realizing key responsibilities in museum work. Each book stands alone, but as a collection they represent a single resource to jump-start the process of pursing best practices and meeting museum standards.

If you are new to working in museums, you may want to read the entire series to get the lay of the land—an overview of what issues you should be aware of and where you can find resources for more information. If you have some museum training but are now responsible for more elements of museum operations than in your previous position, you may start with just the books or chapters covering unfamiliar territory. (You might be wishing you had taken a class in fundraising right about now!) As you prepare to tackle new challenges, we hope that you will refer back to a chapter to orient yourself.

While any chapter can be helpful if read in isolation, we suggest that you start with the first book, *Leadership, Mission, and Governance*, and look at the issues of mission, planning, and assessment. You will find that almost every chapter asks you to consider its subject in light of your mission and make decisions based on it. As you begin to feel overwhelmed by all the possible opportunities and challenges you face, assessment and planning will help you focus your scarce resources strategically—where you need them the most and where they can produce the biggest impact on your organization. And this book offers tips for good governance—defining the role of a trustee and managing the director-trustee relationship. Understanding this relationship from the outset will prevent many headaches down the road.

Financial Resource Development and Management offers you direction about how to raise and manage money and stay within your legal boundaries as a nonprofit. How to manage resources, human and inanimate, effectively and efficiently is discussed in *Organizational Management. Reaching and Responding to the Audience* encourages you to examine your museum audiences and make them comfortable, program to their needs and interests, and spread the word about your good work.

The remaining two books explore the museum foundational concepts of interpretation and stewardship in a small museum setting. *Interpretation: Education, Programs, and Exhibits* considers researching and designing exhibits and best practices for sharing the stories with your audiences. *Stewardship: Collections and Historic Preservation* rounds out the six-book series with an in-depth look at collections care, management, and planning.

We would like to thank the staff at the American Association for State and Local History and AltaMira Press, our families, and our colleagues for encouraging us to pursue this project. You have tirelessly offered your support, and we are incredibly grateful.

There is little reward for writing in service to the museum field—and even less time to do it when you work in a small museum. The contributors to this series generously carved time out of their work and personal lives to share with you their perspectives and lessons learned from years of experience. While not all of them currently hang their hats in small museums, every one of them has worked with or for a small museum and values the incredible work small museums accomplish every day. We offer each and every one of them more appreciation than we can put into words.

We hope that this series makes your lives—as small museum directors, board members, and paid and unpaid staff members—just a little bit easier. We hope that we have gathered helpful perspectives and pointed you in the direction of useful resources.

And when you are faced with a minor annoyance, a major disaster, or just one too many surprises, remember why you do this important work and that you are not alone.

It takes a very special kind of person to endure and enjoy this profession for a lifetime. Not a day passes in which I do not learn something, or find something, or teach something, or preserve something, or help someone.

—Unknown author

Keep up the good work!

Cinnamon Catlin-Legutko
Stacy Lynn Klingler
Editors

PREFACE

I have a confession to make. Until I got to the American Association for State and Local History (AASLH), I never truly understood what it was to work in a small museum. Sure, I had been around them, visited them, talked to my peers who worked in them both as paid and unpaid (read: volunteer) staff, and appreciated the role they play in the historical narrative and in communities. But I never *got it* until I got to AASLH.

So what have I learned? First and foremost, small museums are the bedrock of the American museum profession. You will not find museums the size of the Smithsonian or historic sites like Gettysburg in every American community, but you will often find a small museum, sometimes more than one. While we in the historical profession talk often about how we are the keepers of the American past, and we are, those who work in the smaller institutions are truly minders of our nation's patrimony and heritage. They care for the objects and history of communities throughout the country, stories that would probably be lost without that care. Quite simply, without small museums, our knowledge of the past, our historical narrative, would be incomplete.

The second thing I have learned, and been truly humbled by, is the passion and dedication small museum professionals and volunteers have for their craft. You will rarely hear small museum professionals complaining about a lack of resources—that is just part and parcel of the task at hand. Instead of attacking a challenge with reasons for why something cannot be done, they redirect their thoughts to how it can be done within the parameters provided. So, small museum professionals are equally comfortable with answering the phone, giving a tour, processing collections, and plunging the occasional toilet (the latter falling into the "other duties as assigned" category in a job description).

And amid all that, small museum professionals keep a great sense of humor. At several gatherings of small museum folks over the years, we have had fun with a game we call "You Know You Work in a Small Museum If . . ." Responses ranged from "A staff meeting consists of all staff members turning around in their office chairs at the same time" to "You're the director, but if you're the first one to work after a snowstorm, you get to shovel the sidewalk and plow the parking lot." But my absolute favorite was "When you walk through the gallery and hear a guest say, 'The staff should really do . . .' and you think, Hey, *I'm my staff!*"

At one time, as Steve Friesen of the Buffalo Bill Museum and Grave notes in chapter 2 of Book 1 of this series, the term *small museum* was used as a pejorative. Small museums were underfunded, under-resourced, and poorly managed. "If they weren't," the thinking went, "they'd be large museums, right?" Wrong. Being small does not mean you aspire to be big or that the institution is small because it is doing something wrong. Smallness has more to do with a spirit and dedication to a certain niche of history, a community, a person, a subject.

I believe the field has moved beyond that prejudice, and small museums are now celebrated. At AASLH we often discuss how much larger museums can learn from smaller institutions about how to serve as effective stewards of their resources and to engage their communities in a deep, meaningful way. There is much to learn from small museums, and our peers and colleagues at those institutions are ever willing to share.

Along this line, I have always found that one of the best things about the museum profession in general is how open it is with regard to sharing ideas and processes and just offering support. In no corner of the field is this more evident than in the world of small museums. Small museum professionals are founts of wisdom and expertise, and every small museum session, luncheon, or affinity event I have been to has been packed, and discussion has been stimulating and often inspiring. In fact, discussion often spills out into the hallways after the formal session has concluded.

But the work I know best is that of the AASLH Small Museums Committee. The editors of this series, Cinnamon Catlin-Legutko and Stacy Klingler, are, respectively, the founding and current chairs of this committee. Under their leadership, a team of small museum folks has completed a set of ambitious goals, including gathering a variety of research and developing a small museum needs assessment, presenting sessions at conferences throughout the country, and raising money for scholarships to send peers to the AASLH annual meeting each year. It is this last item I want to highlight as it gives the clearest example of the love and commitment those in small museums have for each other.

In my view, the fact that the Small Museums Committee successfully organizes an annual fundraising campaign is commendable. The fact that it routinely raises money to send *two* people to the meeting (and four people in some years) is truly remarkable. This is indicative of the passion and dedication small museum professionals feel toward the cause of small museums and toward their colleagues. Let's face it, history professionals are not at the top of the salary food chain. (I always note this whenever I speak to history classes about a career in public history. "If you choose this career, you are going to love what you do; you are going to be making a difference in your community. But you are also taking a vow of poverty. No one goes into the history field to get rich.") And while donors to this fund are not all from small museums, small museum professionals are a large part of the pool, giving as generously as anyone. I am so heartened each year as we raise this money.

So, what does all this have to do with the book in your hands? I would say a lot. First, the contributors are small museum professionals or aficionados themselves. They are dedicated to the craft in the small museum environment and know firsthand its needs and challenges. In addition, they have been involved with, and led national discussions on, these issues. They are passionate about the cause of small museums, and they have organized and written a book (and series) that offers a variety of voices and contexts while speaking to the needs as articulated. The thirty-plus contributors to this series offer a wealth of experience and expertise in dealing with the complex nature of running a small museum, in preserving traces of the American past for future generations, often on a shoestring budget and with limited resources. It is a lesson we can all learn. And it is a lesson well articulated here.

Whether you are a seasoned small museum professional, a newly minted executive director, or a museum studies or public history student, it is my hope that this book series will give you the tools you need to succeed in your job. I also hope that you will continue to carry the torch for small museums in your community and in the larger museum field. The field needs your passion and expertise, and the role you fill in your community is critical.

Bob Beatty
Vice President, AASLH

ASSESSMENT TOOLS FOR ADVANCING YOUR MUSEUM

Throughout this book series, you will see references to three assessment programs that small museums are using to advance their organizations—the Standards and Excellence Program for History Organizations (StEPs), the Museum Assessment Program (MAP), and the Conservation Assessment Program (CAP). Each of these programs benefits from funding from the Institute of Museum and Library Services (IMLS) and is designed for museums of all types. And each aligns with widely accepted best practices in the museum field.

These assessment programs are presented here by museum practitioners who manage, or have managed, them. Additionally, museum accreditation is profiled to give you a clear view of how these assessment tools can provide stepping-stones toward museum accreditation. Ultimately, it is our hope, as editors, that you will use these tools to ease your burden and to allocate resources strategically.

Introduction to the StEPs Program

Cherie Cook

In my twenty-plus years working for the Oklahoma Field Advisory Service, the Oklahoma Museums Association, and now the American Association for State and Local History (AASLH), one challenge I have always noted is getting information about appropriate policies and practices into the hands of the wonderful people who operate our nation's local history museums, historic houses and sites, and historical societies. For the most part, they will not find an abundance of this information in local bookstores or libraries, and rarely do they have access within their own communities to this specialized training. *The Small Museum Toolkit* gathers years of experience and expertise from people who understand daily challenges faced by small and extrasmall sites and packages it neatly into a wonderful new series, making the search for the right information much easier. *The Small Museum Toolkit* is a timely resource for all local history organizations, including those enrolled in AASLH's new Standards and Excellence Program for History Organizations, or StEPs.

A self-study program for museums, historic houses and sites, historical societies, and other organizations, StEPs encourages awareness and achievement of national standards. Organizations that enroll in StEPs use standards, self-assessment questions, and performance indicators (basic, good, better) to rate their policies and practices in six sections:

1. Mission, Vision, and Governance
2. Audience
3. Interpretation
4. Stewardship of Collections
5. Stewardship of Historic Structures and Landscapes
6. Management

An organization can address the sections in any order and at its own pace. As a participating organization completes projects, such as adopting a collections management policy or creating an orientation manual for governing authority members, it moves up the performance indicator ladder from "basic" to "good," for example. Once the organization is meeting all "basic" performance indicators in a section, it can report its progress to AASLH and receive a bronze certificate. The same applies for the "good" (silver) and "better" (gold) performance indicators, thus making a total of eighteen certificates available for the organization to earn. Certificates present an opportunity for an organization to be recognized for its accomplishments.

"It was wonderful to see our hard work pay off when we earned a Gold certificate in the Mission, Vision, and Governance section," reported Charlene Orr, executive director of Historic Mesquite in Mesquite, Texas. "StEPs showed us we're on the right track, and more importantly, it made our board of directors understand there's a reason why we have to pay attention to these things. The board was so excited to see our first certificate. It has motivated them to keep going and tackle the next section," she added.

On a broader level, participation in StEPs offers valuable benefits that can be critical to the long-term health and sustainability of an organization. StEPs helps organizations identify potential improvements, provides a mechanism for steering paid and unpaid staff and governing authority members in the same direction, and puts into place an often needed structure for long-term planning. Sara Markoe Hanson, executive director of the White Bear Lake Area Historical Society in White Bear Lake, Minnesota, a site that helped pilot StEPs, commented that the program "spurred us into doing a strategic plan which we had neglected for several years."

Moreover, participation in StEPs helps everyone within an organization learn more about standards. Greater standards awareness and education can extend beyond the walls of the institution via news releases and other communications so that the community learns about national museum standards as well. As an organization takes part in StEPs and begins applying the standards to planning and decision-making, those processes become more meaningful because they are based on practices sanctioned by the museum community and connect the organization to something much larger than itself. This can be particularly helpful when an organization needs to make changes that are unpopular, perhaps due to long-held traditions, but necessary.

Making the case to an organization's governing authority, as well as to funders and donors, for financial and other support for staffing, training, materials, equipment, and services is better justified when requests are directly connected to StEPs and national standards. Flavia Cigliano, executive director of the Nichols House Museum in Boston, another pilot site, reported that the Nichols House applied for and received a grant from IMLS to fund the development of a new interpretive plan. Cigliano's proposal referenced her site's participation in both StEPs and the American Association of Museums' (AAM) Museum Assessment Program (MAP) and integrated her project goals with standards and performance indicators from the StEPs program. "With the basic, good, and better levels, StEPs became a valuable educational experience for us and helped us set goals for the future," she said.

Enrollment in StEPs also leads to increased credibility for the organization within its community and within the museum community. An organization that can track, measure, and articulate its accomplishments within the context of national standards is well prepared to tell its story, gain new supporters, and justify its goals. "It's good to have a national organization like AASLH telling us what we're doing right so we can demonstrate to our county officials that we are following museum standards," says Rob Orrison, historic site manager at Brentsville Courthouse Historic Centre, Bristow, Virginia, one of the first sites to earn StEPs certificates.

Finally, StEPs prepares organizations to take part in other assessment programs like AAM's MAP and Accreditation programs, should they choose to do so. This is especially beneficial for the small and extra-small museums and sites that previously felt ill prepared to take part in a national assessment program. StEPs is the new entry point for these organizations. Upon receiving her site's first gold certificate, Susan Reidy, museum director at Darnall's Chance House Museum, Maryland–National Capital Park and Planning Commission in Upper Marlboro, Maryland, commented, "StEPs is helping us identify our strengths and weaknesses in order to prepare our site to take part in accreditation."

Program History

The StEPs program traces its beginnings to AASLH's Historic House Museums Committee. In April 2002, AASLH and the National Trust for Historic Preservation convened a meeting at Kykuit, the historic Rockefeller estate, near Tarrytown, New York, that brought together twenty-seven representatives of house museums and staff from AASLH, the national trust, AAM, IMLS, and state and regional organizations. While the purpose of the meeting was to address critical issues facing historic house museums, the discussion quickly evolved to include issues relevant not only to house museums but to small history organizations in general. From that meeting, AASLH formed a task force to explore the creation of a program that would raise awareness of national standards and help history organizations achieve them incrementally—that is, one step at a time. AASLH president and CEO Terry Davis notes,

> For many years the field of state and local history has struggled without a roadmap for planning and improvement. The MAP and Accreditation programs offered by AAM have, in the past, been the primary alternatives. As helpful as these extraordinary programs are, they are designed for the museum field, not for the history field and not for small and often all-volunteer organizations. History is different from art or science, and history organizations need standards that stretch the breadth of the field from archives to living history

sites and from local historical societies to military museums. History organizations tell the stories of the past to set the stage for the stories of the future. In doing so, they utilize a unique style of interpretation, historic structures and landscapes, artifacts, and archives. *History is different*, and it deserves its own roadmap to improvement.

In 2005, IMLS awarded AASLH a 21st Century Museum Professionals Grant to develop a standards program for small to midsized history organizations. Early on, project staff and volunteers agreed the program would be built on the core principles of

- promoting and advancing standards awareness;
- focusing on the needs of small and midsized history organizations but opening the program to all organizations;
- offering a voluntary program;
- allowing participants to work toward excellence one section at a time;
- building a program that encourages improvement and rewards progress;
- inviting state, regional, and national service organizations to help in the delivery of program services to their constituents;
- complementing rather than competing with programs offered by other associations, including AAM's MAP and Accreditation programs;
- using standards already employed by AAM to create a seamless structure of improvement in the museum community while recognizing that AASLH would need to add standards to its program to reflect issues specific to history organizations;
- recognizing that the standards will need periodic review and possible revisions.

These important tenets have guided project staff and volunteers throughout the development of StEPs and will continue to help AASLH shape the program as it grows.

Volunteers played a critical role in the IMLS grant project as more than 130 people from across the country enthusiastically donated their time over a four-year period to create the new StEPs program. Task force, committee, and team members spent countless hours designing the program, debating definitions, compromising on performance indicators, vetting the workbook, and, of course, coordinating schedules so busy people could meet via conference call or in Nashville, Phoenix, Boston, Rochester, or wherever else AASLH or AAM

STEPS TASK FORCE, COMMITTEES, TEAMS, PILOTS, AND PROJECT STAFF

StEPs was developed with grant funds from the Institute of Museum and Library Services between 2005 and 2009. AASLH thanks the following volunteers and institutions for their time and expertise given to the project:

Task Force
Bob Beatty, AASLH (Tennessee)
Brian Crockett, Mid-America Arts Alliance HELP Program and consultant (New Mexico)
Terry Davis, AASLH (Tennessee)
Prudence Haines, Shofuso Japanese House and Garden (Pennsylvania)
Julie Hart, American Association of Museums (Washington, DC) (since April 2008)
Katherine Kane, Harriet Beecher Stowe Center (Connecticut)
Janice Klein, formerly at the Mitchell Museum (Illinois) and representing AAM's Small Museums Committee; now a consultant (Arizona)
Ann Korzeniewski, Colvin Run Mill Historic Site, Fairfax County Park Authority, and representing the Small Museum Association (Virginia)
Matt Mayberry, Colorado Springs Pioneers Museum (Colorado)
Elizabeth Merritt, American Association of Museums (Washington, DC) (through April 2008)
Nina Zannieri, Paul Revere Memorial Association (Massachusetts), task force chair

Staff
Cherie Cook, AASLH

Structure and Process Committee
Margo Carlock, Virginia Association of Museums (Virginia)
Brian Crockett, Mid-America Arts Alliance HELP Program and consultant (New Mexico), cochair
Karen Everingham, formerly at Illinois Association of Museums (Illinois)
Jeff Larrabee, formerly at National Guard Bureau (Washington, DC), cochair (through January 2008)
Roger Lidman, Pueblo Grande Museum (Arizona)
Julie Mulvihill, Kansas Humanities Council (Kansas)
Jack Nokes, formerly at Texas Association of Museums (Texas) (through December 2007)

Stephen Patrick, formerly at City of Bowie Museum and Association of Railway Museums (Maryland) (through August 2007)
Mary Turner, formerly at Illinois Association of Museums (Illinois) (through December 2007)

Sustainability Committee
Cinnamon Catlin-Legutko, formerly at General Lew Wallace Study & Museum (Indiana) and representing the AASLH Small Museums Committee; now at Abbe Museum (Maine)
Monta Lee Dakin, Mountain-Plains Museums Association (Colorado)
Brenda Granger, Oklahoma Museums Association (Oklahoma)
Jeff Harris, Indiana Historical Society (Indiana)
Matt Mayberry, Colorado Springs Pioneers Museum (Colorado), chair

Training and Assistance Committee
J. D. Britton, formerly at the Ohio Historical Society (Ohio)
Mark Howell, Howell Consulting (Virginia) and American Civil War Center (Virginia)
Ryan Lewis, Illinois Humanities Council (Illinois)
Patricia Miller, Illinois Heritage Association (Illinois), cochair
Rhonda Newton, Pennsylvania Heritage Society (Pennsylvania)
Karla Nicholson, formerly at the Kentucky Historical Society (Kentucky); now at Liberty Hall Historic Site (Kentucky)
Kate Viens, formerly at New England Museum Association (Massachusetts), cochair

Standards Committee
Prudence Haines, Shofuso Japanese House and Garden (Pennsylvania), cochair
Ann Korzeniewski, Colvin Run Mill Historic Site, Fairfax County Park Authority (Virginia), cochair

Mission, Vision, and Governance Team
Tiffany Davis, College Park Aviation Museum (Maryland)
Theresa Hanley, Ontario Museum of History & Art (California)
Scott Harris, New Market Battlefield State Historical Park (Virginia)
Martha Morris, George Washington University (Washington, DC)
Pat Murphy, Oberlin Heritage Center (Ohio)
John Verrill, City of Manassas (Virginia), team leader
Arthur Wolf, consultant (Nevada)

(*continued*)

Audience Team
Max van Balgooy, National Trust for Historic Preservation (Washington, DC)
Jane Blankman-Hetrick, formerly at Conner Prairie (Indiana) (through March 2007)
Conny Graft, Colonial Williamsburg (Virginia), team leader
Alexandra Rasic, Homestead Museum (California)
Beverly Sheppard, Institute for Learning Innovation (Maryland)
David Simmons, Wade House (Wisconsin)
Marilyn Solvay, Sullivan Museum & History Center (Vermont)
Beth Twiss-Garitty, University of the Arts (Pennsylvania)

Interpretation Team
Kyle Bagnall, Chippewa Nature Center (Michigan)
Katie Boardman, consultant (New York), team leader
Jan Luth, formerly at Heritage Village (Florida)
David Oberg, Geneva History Center (Illinois)
Jane Pieplow, Churchill County Museum (Nevada)
Leslie Przybylek, Mid-America Arts Alliance (Missouri)
Cynthia Robinson, Tufts University and consultant (Massachusetts)
Jennifer Weiskotten, Virginia Association of Museums (Virginia)

Stewardship of Collections Team
Katie Anderson, formerly at the Bead Museum (Arizona); now at Musical Instrument Museum (Arizona)
Erica Huyler Donnis, consultant (Vermont)
Marshall Duell, Old Courthouse Museum (California)
Ellen Endslow, Chester County Historical Society (Pennsylvania)
Stephanie Gaub, Orange County Regional History Center (Florida)
Sue Hanna, Pennsylvania Historical and Museum Commission (Pennsylvania), co–team leader
Melissa Heaver, Fire Museum (Maryland)
Mark Heppner, Stan Hywet Hall and Gardens (Ohio)
Janice Klein, formerly at the Mitchell Museum (Illinois); now a consultant (Arizona)
Claudia Leister, Delaware Division of Historical & Cultural Affairs (Delaware)
Allyn Lord, Shiloh Museum of Ozark History (Arkansas)
Patricia Miller, Illinois Heritage Association (Illinois)
Brenda Reigle, Pennsylvania Historical and Museum Commission (Pennsylvania), co–team leader

Stewardship of Historic Structures and Landscapes Team

Jo Antonson, Alaska Office of History and Archaeology (Alaska), team leader (2007–2008)

Katie Boardman, consultant (New York), co-team leader (2008–2009)

T. Patrick Brennan, Georgia Trust for Historic Preservation (Georgia) (2007–2008)

Susan Edwards, Trustees of Reservations (Massachusetts) (2007–2008)

Doris Devine Fanelli, Independence National Historical Park (Pennsylvania) (2008–2009)

Prudence Haines, Shofuso Japanese House and Garden (Pennsylvania), co-team leader (2008–2009)

Mike Henry, Colvin Run Mill Historic Site, Fairfax County Park Authority (Virginia) (2007–2008)

Carter Lively, Hammond-Harwood House Association (Maryland) (2007–2008)

John Lovell, Bureau of Historic Sites, New York State Office of Parks, Recreation and Historic Preservation (New York) (2008–2009)

Harry P. Lynch, Stan Hywet Hall and Gardens (Ohio) (2007–2008)

Jay Vogt, South Dakota Historical Society (South Dakota) (2007–2009)

Charlotte Whitted, Historic Crab Orchard Museum (Virginia) (2007–2008)

Management Team

Sarah Brophy, consultant (Maryland)

Bob Brown, Historical Museum at Ft. Missoula (Montana)

Ellie Caston, Baylor University (Texas)

Stephen Hague, formerly at Stenton (Pennsylvania)

Lynne Ireland, Nebraska State Historical Society (Nebraska)

Cheryl Kennedy, Early American Museum (Illinois), team leader

Special Projects

Laura Roberts, Tufts University and consultant (Massachusetts); author of Middletown Historical Society case study stories

Kate Theimer, archivist and ArchivesNext blogger (Pennsylvania); consultation on standards and performance indicators that address institutional archives and records retention was holding its annual meeting. Supported by the hard and creative work of many hands, IMLS funding, and enthusiasm from the museum community, StEPs was created by the field for the field.

Pilot Phase

Key to the development of StEPs was the pilot phase involving forty-seven museums, historic sites, and historic houses from across the country. To ensure diversity among the pilots, organizations were selected based on a grid of qualifications, including location, type, annual budget, and paid or unpaid staff size. Each pilot site chose or was assigned one of the six standards workbook sections to address during the test phase. After reviewing self-assessment questions and performance indicators in its workbook section, each pilot site then planned and completed one or more projects that would move it closer to achieving standards in that section.

In Minnesota, staff from the Bois Forte Heritage Center spent a day at the Minnesota Historical Society learning how to make storage mounts for ethnographic artifacts as they tested the "Stewardship of Collections" section. Upon completion of the pilot phase, Bill Latady, Bois Forte Heritage Center curator, reported, "The workbook provided an excellent resource for evaluating our entire program. Summarizing standards within broad categories of institutional achievement and providing a methodical approach does indeed promote improvement at a pace that a small staff with limited resources can follow. Furthermore, in an institutional environment where the governing body has limited experience with historical institutions, a nonjudgmental step-by-step process embodied in a workbook serves as a teaching aid and measuring standard."

In addition to the forty-seven sites, the pilot phase involved eleven service organizations also selected according to a grid of qualifications. The service organizations, like the Minnesota Historical Society's Office of Outreach Services, which arranged for the Bois Forte Heritage Center's staff training, provided information, guidance, and instruction to the five or six pilot sites located within their states or regions.

Another pilot service organization, the California Association of Museums, coordinated a one-day workshop for its pilot sites, all of which focused on the "Interpretation" section of the StEPs workbook. Six sites in Texas, under the guidance of the Texas Historical Commission and the Texas Association of Museums, received training online by taking part in AASLH's "Basics of Archives" course and then applying that knowledge to a project focused on improving collections care at each site.

Some pilot service organizations had the resources to send a staff member to each of their pilot sites for a one-on-one meeting. Both the Ohio Historical

StEPs PILOT PHASE

A variety of small and mid-sized history organizations from across the country piloted the StEPs workbook from March through September 2008. To ensure diversity among the pilots, the Training and Assistance Committee chose the forty-seven sites based on a grid of qualifications, including location, type, annual budget, and paid or unpaid staff size. Each pilot site chose or was assigned one section of the workbook to address during the test phase. After reviewing the standards, self-assessment questions, and performance indicators, each pilot site then undertook one or more projects to move them closer to achieving standards in their chosen section.

In addition to the sites, the pilot phase involved service organizations also chosen according to a grid of qualifications. The service organizations provided information and training to the five or six pilot sites located within the service organization's state or region. The purpose of the pilot phase was to test the effectiveness of the StEPs materials. More specifically, the purpose was to determine the degree to which the program achieved the following outcomes:

1. It increased awareness about and the value of national standards among the pilot sites.
2. It increased the belief that all history museums should strive to meet national standards.
3. It increased the knowledge and skills of staff and/or volunteers in the program section addressed during the pilot phase.

A comparison of the results of the pre- and postpilot surveys showed that each of the above outcomes exhibited an increase.

Of the sites, 92 percent (forty-three) completed the pilot phase. AASLH defined completion as responding to contact from AASLH and the service organization assigned to help the site and facilitating evaluation activities by taking the postpilot survey, participating in a conference call, submitting a brief final report, and returning the pilot workbook. All of the service organizations completed the project. Service organizations and pilot sites that completed the program included the following:

Mid-Atlantic Region
Service organization:
Delaware Museum Association and Small Museum Association, Amanda Apple, Claudia Leister, Mary Wagner, and Pam Williams

(continued)

11

TEXTBOX 1.2 (Continued)

Pilot sites:
Lewes Historical Society, Lewes, Delaware; Mike DiPaolo
Mount Clare Museum House, Baltimore, Maryland; Abbi Wicklein-Bayne
Queen Anne's Museum of Eastern Shore Life, Centreville, Maryland; Ma-
   rie Malaro
Rose Hill Manor Park & Children's Museum, Frederick, Maryland; Jen-
   nifer Roth
Seaford Historical Society, Seaford, Delaware; Sharlana Edgell

Midwest Region
Service organization:
Ohio Historical Society, J. D. Britton

Pilot sites:
Canfield Historical Society, Canfield, Ohio; Suzie McCabe
Clinton County Historical Society, Wilmington, Ohio; Kay Fisher
National Cambridge Glass Museum, Cambridge, Ohio; Sharon Miller
North Canton Heritage Society, North Canton, Ohio; Kathleen Fernandez
Sandusky Library/Follett House Museum, Sandusky, Ohio; Maggie Marconi

Mountain-Plains Region
Service organizations:
Texas Historical Commission, Laura Casey
Texas Association of Museums, Jack Nokes and Ruth Ann Rugg

Pilot sites:
Brownsville Heritage Complex, Brownsville, Texas; Jessica Villescaz
Denton County Museums, Denton, Texas; Kim McCoig Cupit
Depot Museum Complex, Henderson, Texas; Susan Weaver
El Paso Museum of History, El Paso, Texas; Barbara Angus
Texas Pharmacy Museum, Amarillo, Texas; Paul Katz
Wolf Creek Heritage Museum, Lipscomb, Texas; Virginia Scott

New England Region
Service organization:
New England Museum Association, Kate Viens

Pilot sites:
American Precision Museum, Windsor, Vermont; Ann Lawless
Belfast Historical Society & Museum, Belfast, Maine; George Squibb
Nichols House Museum, Boston, Massachusetts; Flavia Cigliano

Pettaquamscutt Historical Society, Kingston, Rhode Island; Liz Holstein and Kathy Bossy

Sandwich Historical Society, Sandwich, New Hampshire; Matthew Powers

Southeast Region

Service organizations:

Mississippi Department of Archives and History, Cindy Gardner

Mississippi Humanities Council, David Morgan

Pilot sites:

Camp Van Dorn WWII Museum, Centreville, Mississippi; Vicki Netterville

Eudora Welty House, Jackson, Mississippi; Amy Steadman

Mississippi Armed Forces Museum, Camp Shelby, Mississippi; James Darrah

Oktibbeha County Heritage Museum, Starkville, Mississippi; Joan Wilson

Pearl River Community College Museum, Poplarville, Mississippi; Ronn Hague

Union County Heritage Museum, New Albany, Mississippi; Jill Smith

West Region

Service organization:

California Association of Museums, Christine Bennett and Sarah Post

Pilot sites:

Agricultural History Project, Watsonville, California; Pat Johns

Eastern California Museum, Independence, California; Roberta Harlan

Jake Jackson Memorial Museum, Weaverville, California; J. Robert Gale and Marilyn Gale

Japanese American Museum of San Jose, San Jose, California; Aggie Idemoto

Kelley House Museum, Mendocino, California; Nancy Freeze

At-Large

Service organization:

Alaska State Museum, Scott Carrlee

Pilot sites:

Baranov Museum, Kodiak, Alaska; Katie Oliver

Cordova Historical Museum, Cordova, Alaska; Cathy Sherman

Hammer Museum, Haines, Alaska; Dave Pahl

Kenai Visitors & Cultural Center, Kenai, Alaska; Laura Forbes

Museum of the Aleutians, Unalaska, Alaska; Zoya Johnson

(*continued*)

Service organization:
Minnesota Historical Society, David Grabitske

Pilot sites:
Bois Forte Heritage Center and Cultural Museum, Tower, Minnesota; Bill Latady
Hennepin County Medical Center Museum, Minneapolis, Minnesota; Suzanne Fischer
Kittson County Historical Society, Lake Bronson, Minnesota; Cindy Adams
Mower County Historical Society, Austin, Minnesota; Kelly Olson and Dustin Heckman
Sacred Heart Area Historical Society, Sacred Heart, Minnesota; Sonja Thune
White Bear Lake Area Historical Society, White Bear Lake, Minnesota; Sara Markoe Hanson

Society and the Mississippi Department of Archives and History arranged half- or full-day training workshops for each of their pilot sites presented either by field service staff or other agency personnel. Others, like Scott Carrlee, curator of museum services at the Alaska State Museum, used telephone and e-mail correspondence to guide his sites, just as he does for most of his day-to-day field service work due to travel limitations that Alaskans routinely face. The two all-volunteer service organizations had a more difficult time serving their pilot sites because their volunteers all hold demanding full-time jobs. This was no surprise to AASLH and pilot phase organizers; it did, however, serve to underline the need to perhaps plan to pay extra attention to states where the capacity level of service organizations is not as high.

Overall, the pilot phase resulted in an increase in participants' knowledge and awareness of national standards and an enthusiastic response from service organizations.

Service Organizations' Continued Key Role

As during the pilot phase, national, state, and regional associations, field service programs, state historical societies, state humanities councils, and other service organizations play an important role in the StEPs program today. They have direct contact with thousands of historical societies, historic houses, and other sites that are not members of AASLH. Moreover, those organizations naturally look to their state museum association, state humanities council, and other local groups for help and advice. AASLH invites service organizations to help spread the word about StEPs so it reaches the local level.

Additionally, service organizations are encouraged to create mentoring programs, annual meeting sessions, user groups, and other programs that help small and midsized museums enrolled in StEPs to network, share issues and resources, obtain support, and stay motivated to complete the program.

AASLH recognizes the outstanding work already being performed by service organizations. But, as mentioned previously, it also understands that capacity (funding, paid and unpaid staff, time, and other precious resources) varies not only at individual museums and sites but also from service organization to service organization. In some states, service organization staff may be available to guide or mentor StEPs participants in a group setting or even one on one, while service organizations in other states have the capacity to do little more than disseminate information about StEPs and encourage enrollment.

Jeff Harris and Stacy Klingler, members of the staff at the Indiana Historical Society's Local History Services department, are using the six StEPs section topics to help them structure their training program calendar for the next several years. They are also using the program's standards and performance indicators to create a prioritizing tool for use by small museums, even those not enrolled in StEPs.

In Alaska, Scott Carrlee is now using StEPs in a variety of ways to help not only local museums and sites enrolled in StEPs but all organizations he serves. For those enrolled in StEPs, Carrlee has formed a users group that meets during the Museums Alaska annual meeting and communicates the rest of the year by phone and e-mail. Nonenrolled organizations that request an on-site consultation from Carrlee benefit indirectly from StEPs because he has incorporated the program's "basic," "good," and "better" performance indicators into both the consultation checklist he uses when he visits museums and sites and the report he sends as a follow-up to the on-site consultation. "The StEPs program is probably the greatest thing to come along for small museums in the last decade or so," says Carrlee. "StEPs is at the core of how I deliver my support to small museums in Alaska."

In the first ten months after StEPs was launched, two states created grant programs offering funding to history organizations wanting to enroll. As part of its Legacy Grants program, the Minnesota Historical Society added a new category in 2010: "Historical Organization Self-Assessment Using StEPs." This new category offers funding not only for enrollment but also for project expenses like hiring a consultant and purchasing supplies. Also in 2010, the Maryland Historical Trust awarded a grant to the Maryland Association of History Museums for the purpose of regranting funds to local organizations for participation in StEPs.

The StEPs Program Today

AASLH will no doubt continue to improve and build on the StEPs program in the years to come. A permanent StEPs Advisory Committee is already in place, and work has begun on a project to create more program resources. This new follow-up project, StEPs Part II, funded by an IMLS 21st Century Museum Professionals Grant, is creating three new program components: a national on-line clearinghouse of resource materials, six standards-related curricula available free of charge to service organizations, and six standards-related webinars that AASLH will offer to the field. Topics for the curricula and webinars include fundraising in tough times, strategic thinking and planning, and drafting a collections management policy. All will be completed by the end of 2012.

Without grant funding from IMLS, the creation of StEPs would not have been possible. AASLH extends thanks to IMLS for funding the project and, for their continued support and encouragement, to former IMLS director Dr. Anne-Imelda Radice; Marsha Semmel, director for strategic partnerships; Mary Estelle Kennelly, grants management officer; and Christopher Reich, associate deputy director for museums.

AASLH also thanks a cast of hundreds, our colleagues from across the nation who worked on the standards project. Due to their efforts, IMLS funding, and support from the museum community, we finally have a program that helps history organizations not only learn about standards but plot a course for improvement and long-term sustainability.

Museum Assessment and Accreditation Programs

Elizabeth Merritt

The Keys to Change

As individuals, we have many options for self-improvement. We can buy a gym membership and hire a personal trainer if we need help sticking with a fitness regime. We can read self-help books, or even see a life coach, to help us reclaim our groove. We can go back to school, signing up for courses to expand our horizons and deepen our knowledge. We can earn degrees or certifications to buff up our resumes, get better jobs, and raise our incomes. It is all hard work, but there is plenty of choice.

Museums have fewer support systems for self-improvement, which is unfortunate because they are in particular need of a helping hand when they want to better themselves. Changing an organization requires changing the knowledge, behaviors, and attitudes of the people who comprise it—a difficult task whether it involves a handful or hundreds of folk. All three of these components are crucial and require a special kind of coaching to coax change.

- *Knowledge* requires mastering information about what to do, when, and how. It presumes some common standards for determining the right course of action.
- *Behaviors* change when people are motivated to move beyond comfortable routines. Positive, internally focused motivation is the strongest incentive. When people have the prospect of accomplishing cherished goals and improving their work conditions, they make the effort to leave their comfort zone and try something new.
- *Attitudes* can be very entrenched. They are often personal, subjective, and unvoiced. People are often tethered to their attitudes by unstated assumptions about how the world works, or how the museum should work, and what will happen if things change. Negative motivation never changes attitudes but only entrenches them further. Attitudes are most likely to change when people have new experiences and are exposed to new perspectives in situations that make them receptive to new ideas.

17

The museum excellence programs of the American Association of Museums are engineered to help change the knowledge, behaviors, and attitudes of staff, board members, and volunteers, enabling museums to raise themselves to a higher level of achievement. The Museum Assessment and Accreditation programs have evolved, over the course of forty years, into tremendously effective tools for museum advancement. This section gives a brief overview of the philosophies and basic methodologies shared by both programs and the specialized ways in which they fill distinct niches.

Capsule Description of the Programs

The museum excellence programs of the American Association of Museums include the Museum Assessment Program and the Accreditation Program, which share the same criteria for evaluation (national standards and best practices) and the same basic program elements (self-assessment and peer review).

Self-assessment, the process by which a museum evaluates its own performance, has several benefits. It establishes a common basis for understanding standards and best practices as applied in the programs. It fosters self-awareness, giving staff, board members, and volunteers the chance to step back from their daily work and reflect on the bigger picture. And it provokes discussion and mutual learning—nothing elucidates how things really work in your museum better than having to capture the process on paper in order to explain it to someone else!

Peer review, provided by museum practitioners who volunteer their time, provides an objective perspective. Sometimes an outsider can see (or say) things that are hidden from the people who work in the museum every day. Peer reviewers can provide a broader context for the museum's evaluation, drawing on experiences at their own institutions and those they have reviewed to benchmark a museum's performance. Perhaps most importantly, the words of a peer reviewer carry the credibility of an outside expert. It is sad but true that often a prophet is without honor in his own land. The on-staff expert may be ignored for years, while the powers that be perk up and pay attention to a peer reviewer offering exactly the same words of wisdom.

Museum Assessment Program

The American Association of Museums has partnered with the Institute for Museum and Library Service since 1981 to provide MAP as a service to the field. IMLS underwrites most of the costs of the program by subsidizing AAM's services, enabling museums to participate with minimal expense. AAM staff create and administer the program, working with museums to counsel them through the process. There are some basic criteria for admission to the program, but participation in MAP is noncompetitive.

In MAP, museum staff complete a self-study that involves answering simple questions about how they operate (e.g., temperature and humidity levels, number of exhibits per year) together with a few essay questions about the museum's mission and values. Staff, board members, and volunteers also undertake scripted activities that provoke discussion, help people see the museum in new ways, and test theory (policies and procedures) against reality (actual daily practice). Museums can choose among several MAP assessments, with different areas of emphasis, and this will determine the focus of the questions and activities.

This self-assessment and some basic documentation, such as the institutional plan and various written policies, are provided to someone from another museum, who volunteers to serve as a peer reviewer. The peer reviewer reads through the self-study, maybe checks out the museum on the Web, and schedules a visit (usually lasting one day) to spend on-site, touring the museum and interviewing staff, board members, and volunteers. During the visit, the peer reviewer finds out more about what museum staff want and need from the assessment. Sometimes the peer reviewer, based on his or her experience and outside perspective, sees problems that the museum has overlooked or avoided and will recommend that the staff rethink their priorities. These observations and recommendations are summarized in a comprehensive report evaluating how well the museum meets national standards and best practices, giving advice about what steps the museum might take next in order to improve, and pointing the museum toward resources that may be of assistance. The museum can use the report in whatever way it sees best: as a public relations tool, sharing the report with the public, funders, and the press; as a roadmap, integrating its recommendations into institutional planning; or as an educational document for staff, board members, and volunteers. In MAP, the museum is the client, and the peer reviewer is there to help in whatever way he or she can. Often the peer reviewer and the museum keep in touch after the assessment and develop a long-term mentor-mentee relationship.

MAP is a great starting point for your museum if you need assistance with identifying strengths and weaknesses, setting priorities, getting everyone in the museum (staff, board members, volunteers) on the same page, making the case for resources for improvement, preparing for accreditation or for institutional change, or getting mentoring and advice.

Accreditation Program

Because the Accreditation Program provides national certification of excellence, it is, by nature, more objective and less warm and fuzzy. The self-study process is more rigorous and in-depth than any one of the MAP reviews, covering every aspect of the museum's operations and digging into all important policies and procedures.

To guard against bias and ensure a balanced perspective, the museum is assigned two peer reviewers. This committee of reviewers visits the museum to check the accuracy of the self-study, make sure it reflects how things really operate, and dig deeper into the story behind the words and the numbers. The client for their report is not the museum but the Accreditation Commission—the body appointed by the AAM board to make decisions regarding museum accreditation. The visiting committee's report captures the reviewers' observations and assessment of how the museum's policies, procedures, and performance meet, or fail to meet, national standards. It does not include recommendations for improvement or for how the museum might address any problems uncovered by the review.

The visiting committee's report is submitted directly to the Accreditation Commission, which makes its decision based on the report as well as the museum's self-study and documentation (yes, they do read it!). The commission can grant or deny accreditation or table its decision in order to give the museum time to fix some things. If the commissioners table their decision, they tell the museum about their concerns and what they want the museum to do. They are not prescriptive in these directives—they will sketch the outcome they want (a policy brought into line with standards, an outline of plans for financial stability), but they will leave the details of how to respond up to the museum.

The vast majority of museums accepted into the Accreditation Program end up becoming accredited—partly because the program staff is really good at counseling museums about whether they are ready to apply and giving advice on what they need to do before diving in. AAM staff often recommend that a museum undertake MAP as a way to get ready for accreditation, using it as a dry run and asking peer reviewers for feedback on what they need to do to prepare for a successful accreditation application. However, it is pretty common for the commission to table decisions and to present museums with a list of anywhere from one to half a dozen things they need to address. Most museums find this phenomenally helpful—often the commission points to things that the director and staff have long wanted to address. Sometimes a finger wag from the commission is just what is needed to break an internal logjam or shake loose the resources needed to get things done.

Once accredited, a museum enters a regular cycle of review and subsequent accreditation to keep its accredited status. This enables the commission to ensure that the museum is maintaining the quality of its performance. And it ensures that the museum is keeping up with evolving standards and best practices, as well as changing its plans and operations to suit its own changing environment.

Accreditation may be the right program for your museum if you have broad involvement and buy-in from all levels of leadership; all your policies and procedures in place, including an institutional plan; the support of your governing authority to make any needed improvements identified in the course of the review; and time to devote to the rigorous process. If you are buffed and ready to shine, accreditation will provide the spotlight for your success.

You do not have to know where your museum fits to enter the continuum of excellence. AAM staff are happy to provide counseling about which program, at AAM or elsewhere, would be the best next step along your pathway to improvement.

National Standards and Best Practices

When the Accreditation Program started in the early 1970s, the reviews were pretty intuitive and informal. A committee of two colleagues visited the museum, looked around, talked to staff, formed their own opinions of whether the museum was up to snuff or not, and wrote a report for the commission. Since being denied accreditation is a big deal, museums were understandably concerned about the basis for these judgments. And the commission struggled to be equitable while weighing visiting committee reports that often differed enormously in what they looked at and what they criticized.

Over time, as the commission conducted dozens, then hundreds, then more than a thousand reviews, it started codifying its decisions in a series of "characteristics" and "expectations," explaining what it looked for in assessing planning, say, or a mission statement, or governance. Nonaccredited museums started looking to these expectations for guidance as well, and they became de facto benchmarks for museum performance. In 2006, the role of the accreditation standards in guiding the field was formalized when the AAM board of trustees designated them "national standards and best practices" for U.S. museums. So, by participating in accreditation, museums join the cadre of institutions that set the pace for all their peers. The best practices of the highest-performing accredited museums are summarized as examples for the field. The commission singles out areas in which even many of the best-performing museums have problems, such as collections planning, for additional attention by AAM through colloquia, seminars, and meeting sessions, fostering a national dialog that in time may lead to the creation of new standards.

Excellence and Small Museums

It is very difficult to develop and apply standards to entities as diverse as museums. The differences in scale (all volunteer to hundreds of paid staff) and scope (historic sites, fine arts institutions, zoos, science centers) are boggling.

Accreditation found the key to evaluating such disparate institutions to be two core questions, one of which is "How well does the museum's performance meet standards and best practices as generally understood in the field and *as appropriate to its circumstances?*"

This means, in effect, that a small museum is not expected to behave like a large museum. It can be excellent in its own way, as is appropriate for its budget and resources. Excellent climate control in a large museum might include state-of-the-art heating, cooling, and humidification systems. Excellent climate control in a small history house might include opening and closing the windows at appropriate times of the day and year, installing and maintaining a portable dehumidifier in storage, and making sure the gutters do not leak.

MAP is explicitly designed to serve the needs of small museums—more than 25 percent of participants have operating expenses of under $125,000, and 50 percent have operating expenses under $400,000. Half of participants have a paid staff of between one and five people, and about one-fifth have one to five full-time, unpaid staff. While there is no minimum budget size for an accredited museum, because of the rigor of the process and the time that it requires, small museums make up proportionately fewer participants in the Accreditation Program than in MAP. In 2010, about 10 percent of accredited museums[1] had annual operating expenses at or below $350,000, and 15 percent had annual operating expenses under $500,000.

Motivation

What are the incentives to undertake a program of self-improvement? The reasons museum staff report for undertaking MAP or the Accreditation Program have remained strikingly consistent over the years and include an interesting mix of tangible and intangible benefits:

- *Excellence:* For nonprofit museums, the ultimate measure of success is their ability to deliver on their mission. And the major driver for museum practitioners is the ability and opportunity to do their best work, which necessitates a continual process of learning and applying the most up-to-date knowledge. Participating in museum excellence programs is the ultimate hands-on tutorial, a chance to really live the standards, which has a much greater impact than reading dry words in a book.
- *Alignment:* Even the shared desire for excellence can cause tension when people have different concepts of what is "good" or "best." The MAP and Accreditation programs provide a common, objective framework for discussion—the national standards and best

practices that underlie both programs. This enables staff to discuss potentially divisive matters with a neutral, directed approach, minimizing the potential personal concerns. And going through a review facilitates the museum's developing shared priorities, moving, as one director put it, from "ambition and confusion" to "a directive and a direction."

- *Accountability:* Many museums enroll in excellence programs to show supporters and funders that the museum is making good use of the resources entrusted to it. MAP demonstrates that the museum is striving to meet national standards and best practices, and the Accreditation Program provides national recognition for having achieved these goals.

- *Resources:* Participating in the excellence programs can yield tangible benefits as well—be they financial, relational, or other. For art museums, for example, accreditation facilitates borrowing from other art museums. Museums that have completed a MAP assessment are better positioned to compete successfully for funds such as the IMLS's Museums for America grants. And the programs foster a rich network of valuable connections as well, particularly with the colleagues who volunteer to conduct the museum's review. As one director put it, this served as both an "antidote to isolation" in a remote, rural institution and as a "therapy session" for staff.

These motivations are echoed on a larger stage for the field as a whole. Through programs such as those described in this book, museums establish their credibility and accountability to the American public, policymakers, and funders. Peer review—the hallmark of the MAP and Accreditation programs—has created a phenomenal professional network of support and mutual education. And taken together, the programs have served as the crucible for the testing and development of standards and best practices for our field. AAM subsidizes accreditation because of these emergent benefits that profit the field as a whole, in addition to the direct benefits experienced by accredited museums.

Lessons from Museum Excellence Programs

Mission

I wrote earlier of one core question from the Accreditation Program, that which puts performance in the context of a museum's resources. The second question is "How well does the museum achieve its stated mission and goals?"

This, in effect, lets a museum set its own benchmark for success. For example, try assessing the success of a small history museum with excellent exhibits and programming and a small collection adequate to its need. If its mission is to serve the local community and provide a good general resource for the local schools, it may be a rousing success. If its mission is to be an internationally acclaimed museum recognized for its historical scholarship, it has quite a ways to go.

A mission statement can generate more angst than any other sentence (or paragraph) the museum staff and board ever write. People can get so heavily invested in the process of crafting the mission and give it such weight and significance that they argue for hours over the placement of a comma. Or they see the inclusion or exclusion of their department, collection, or area of expertise as an indicator of their status and security in the museum. To avoid these painful situations, it can help to step back and take a cool look at the function of the statement.

At its heart, the mission statement exists to explain why the museum matters and to whom. It answers the question, "How is the world any different because this museum exists?" This sentiment is encapsulated in the national standard's "characteristics of excellence" as "the museum has a clear understanding of its mission and communicates why it exists and who benefits as a result of its work." In both the MAP and Accreditation programs, peer reviewers and the commission will refer to the mission statement constantly in the course of a review, assessing a museum's choices in light of this overarching goal.

This being so, museums often begin their preparation for either program with an internal look at their mission statement, evaluating whether it really captures what they mean to achieve and whether it is perhaps either too modest or too ambitious in scope. Sometimes the peer reviewer or the commission may suggest this later on in the process. There are occasional epiphanies in the programs in which a museum realizes that its operations are just fine; it need only bring its ambitions (as captured in the mission statement) into alignment with what it can actually achieve. The museum may realize that the more ambitious statement is a future goal rather than a present criterion against which it should be judged and turn it into a vision statement to guide planning.

Another common experience is for museums to find, as they compile their self-studies, that more than one version of the mission statement exists, embedded in various documents like a fossil record of the museum's development over time. One fringe benefit of the thorough review of policies and procedures occasioned by the programs is to make sure all these documents are up to date and in alignment.

Finally, MAP and Accreditation reviews are an opportunity for museums that exist within larger parent organizations (such as a university or city government) to make sure everyone is still on the same page regarding the museum's purpose and function. Unfortunately, this cannot be taken for granted.

If the museum staff wrote the mission statement, it may never truly have come to the attention of those in real authority, up a complex organizational chain, and may not have their support. If a remote supervisor or governing group in the organization developed the mission statement, it may be unrealistic or out of synch with the museum's true promise and capabilities. Because representatives from the parent organization will be involved in the review, at some level, this is a chance to command the attention of the museum's overseers and to ensure that everyone has truly bought into the mission and accepts it as a valid measure of success.

Governance

It is a paradox of our profession that trained professionals are accountable to people with passion, and ideally the resources to support the museum, who are often highly trained in their own professions but rarely have any training in nonprofit management or museum standards. For this reason, in the realm of governance the educational potential of the MAP and Accreditation programs truly shines. Governing authorities get emotionally and intellectually engaged in the process of getting an IMLS MAP grant or becoming accredited. Therefore, once a museum is in an excellence program, it becomes easier to bring the governing authority into the process of discussing standards, particularly as they pertain to the governing authorities' responsibility. Sometimes, a MAP assessment is a board member's first exposure to a formal list of what those legal responsibilities are!

Sometimes the museum's self-study quickly reveals that basic documentation regarding governance is not in place. Can the museum assemble its mission statement, institutional plan, founding documents (articles of incorporation, charter, enabling legislation, or other), bylaws, constitution, or other documentation under which the museum is governed? If the museum exists inside a larger parent organization, is there documentation regarding the importance of the museum to the parent, expressing the parent's commitment to provide support? If the museum has separately incorporated support groups or is jointly operated by more than one legal entity, are there agreements spelling out the obligations of these relationships? Has the governing authority formally and appropriately delegated authority to the director for the day-to-day operation of the museum? The process of assembling and reviewing these core documents and ensuring that they are internally consistent and up to date is laborious and sometimes contentious. It may take the impetus of a formal, external review to ensure that this happens.

The MAP and Accreditation programs can also impel a museum's governing authority to pay attention to some of the even harder and subtler problems of governance: diversity and succession planning. National standards regarding the appropriate composition of a museum's staff and board are still evolving. But there is an emerging consensus that it is appropriate for the board and staff to reflect the museum's community. While the standards are general and nonprescriptive in this regard, self-study and peer review may bring up tough questions about where the next generation of board members will come from, how they will be recruited, and how they will help the museum remain sustainable in the long term. Currently, one MAP assessment looks specifically at governance and engages members of the governing authority in activities and questions related to their roles and responsibilities. Members of the visiting accreditation committee will meet with at least the chair of the board (or someone with equivalent authority in a parent organization), if not the full board of trustees. Personal engagement with the review process can be educational and engaging for members of the governing authority and can provide the necessary stimulus for changes that require support from the very top.

Summary

The museum excellence programs of the American Association of Museums have been honed over the course of decades to provide effective ways to change the knowledge, behaviors, and attitudes of those guiding and operating museums. By providing positive motivation in the form of opportunities to do good work, access resources, demonstrate accountability, and align the efforts of everyone involved, the programs offer an effective mechanism for harnessing the energy, enthusiasm, and talent of museum board members, staff, and volunteers. By grounding their assessments in national standards and best practices, they provide a common framework for excellence. By combining the strengths of self-assessment and peer review, they deepen self-awareness and place the museum's achievements in a broader context. Whether undertaken separately or in sequence, and together with the other programs outlined in this book, they offer museums a clear pathway to achieving success.

The Conservation Assessment Program

Sara Gonzales

Imagine it is your first week on the job as the collections manager of a small local history museum. After touring the site and reviewing the institution's policies, plans, and procedures manuals, you feel a small twinge of panic. The museum has been collecting items for thirty years with the only collections policy being "the artifact has to relate to the history of the local community," regardless of size, the existence of duplicates in the collection, or insect infestations. Dedicated storage areas exist, but you find evidence of mold and pests and a lack of proper environmental controls. To top it off, as a three-day-per-week employee, you have no idea how you will find the time and money to address these collections issues—you will be too busy keeping the doors open, running educational programs, and producing four new temporary exhibits each year. How will these urgent conservation needs ever be addressed?

Museum staff who find themselves in the above scenario can be assured that they are not alone. According to the findings of the Heritage Health Index (a 2004 survey of all collecting institutions in the United States conducted by Heritage Preservation in partnership with IMLS), there are 12,057 museums in the United States and 3,303 historical societies. Of the combined 15,360 museums and historical societies, 1,336 (9 percent) are large, 1,864 (12 percent) are medium sized, and 12,160 (79 percent) are small.[2] The majority of these small institutions report need for improvement in all aspects of preventive conservation, including storage furniture and equipment, storage space, environmental controls, and preventive conservation training opportunities for employees. Often lacking training in the fundamentals of conservation, as well as in fundraising and grant writing, staff members at these museums frequently do not know where to start on their quest to improve collections stewardship.

The Conservation Assessment Program helps to meet these needs by providing small museums with a background in preventive conservation fundamentals and a roadmap for conservation planning and fundraising. CAP addresses the full range of preventive conservation needs of museum collections and outlines methods to improve collections care and preservation in the long term. To achieve this goal, CAP matches museums with qualified professionals who assess institutions and provide prioritized recommendations for increasing museum standards. For many small museums, assessments through CAP and MAP are the first steps on the road toward achieving professional museum standards and best practices and, in some cases, accreditation.

What Is CAP?

The Conservation Assessment Program was developed in 1989 in response to a 1984–1985 survey on the preventive conservation needs of U.S. museums conducted by the American Association of Museums.[3] The study found that 30 percent of museums had surveyed none of their collections and that 36 percent had surveyed less than half of their collections. Furthermore, 72 percent of museums had no long-range plan for the conservation of their collections. These findings documented the fact, widely discussed in the field, that museums with smaller budgets had fewer abilities to address the conservation of their collections. The Institute of Museum Services therefore introduced CAP in 1990 to provide grants to small museums for a general assessment of preventive conservation practices. Today, CAP continues as a technical assistance program supported by IMLS through a cooperative agreement with Heritage Preservation, a national nonprofit organization dedicated to preserving the cultural heritage of the United States.

The CAP assessment consists of three portions: completion of a site questionnaire detailing current collections practices at the institution, a site visit and survey of collections conservation conditions by a trained conservator (and a building preservation survey by a historic structure assessor if the museum maintains a building fifty years old or older), and review and receipt of a report from each assessor containing a description of current conditions at the institu-

---

TEXTBOX 1.3

WHEN IS THE RIGHT TIME FOR A CAP ASSESSMENT?

If the museum does not have a current assessment on file, then any time is a good time for a conservation assessment. However, there are certain times in an organization's life cycle when an assessment can be particularly beneficial:

- Just before creating or updating the strategic plan
- Immediately following a period of institutional change (staff turnover, board adjustments, etc.) so the staff will have a new, common starting point
- When potential grants have been identified and conservation plans need to be solidified for the application
- When past grant applications have been turned down due to a lack of a prioritized list of conservation needs

tion and a list of prioritized recommendations for improving long-term preservation. The assessment is funded in large part by an allocation from Heritage Preservation. As part of the museum's commitment to the assessment, a small amount of organizational funds should be budgeted to supplement the CAP allocation in order to meet the assessor's professional fees and travel expenses.

The CAP Assessors

Heritage Preservation maintains a list of more than four hundred assessors for the Conservation Assessment Program. Collections assessors are professionals who have earned a master's degree in conservation or obtained extensive conservation training through apprenticeship. Although their specialties vary from paintings to works on paper, to wooden objects/furniture, to textiles, they all possess the ability to assess conditions at small museums with any type of nonliving collections within two days and write a report containing recommendations for improving collection preservation practices.

Historic structure assessors may be architects or historic preservationists trained to the master's level in the conservation of historic structures. Living collections assessors are either professional zoologists or horticulturalists with experience conducting general assessments of institutions with living collections. Assessor applications are carefully reviewed by Heritage Preservation in order to ensure that qualified professionals with experience conducting general assessments are approved to perform CAP assessments.[4]

Participation in CAP

Application and Eligibility

The CAP cycle begins each fall and runs for one year. Applications are made available on Heritage Preservation's website in October.[5] The deadline to apply is December 1. The application requires submission of a tally of all collections items held by the museum (by type of object) and basic information about the institution's building. Applicants should be prepared to list the name, duties, and weekly schedule of all museum staff who perform professional functions (museum administrative, curatorial, and educational duties are considered professional functions).

In order to be eligible for CAP, the applicant institution must meet IMLS's definition of a museum: The institution must be

- either a unit of state or local government or a private not-for-profit organization that has tax-exempt status under the Internal Revenue Code;

ITEMS TO HAVE ON HAND TO COMPLETE THE CAP APPLICATION

- A photocopy of the museum's 501(c)(3) letter from the IRS or, for museums that are a unit of local, state, or tribal government, a letter identifying the museum as a unit of government on the government entity's letterhead and signed by an official of that entity.
- A Dun and Bradstreet (DUNS) number (available at www.dnb.com).
- Contact information for an authorizing official from the museum's board of directors or equivalent governing body (the authorizing official may not be the museum's director or the project contact); the authorizing official must also provide an original signature on the application.
- A list of all the staff along with their responsibilities and hours worked per week.
- A list of all the museum's buildings along with maintenance and repair logs. If the building has undergone a historic structures report in the past, have that report available.
- The museum's previous CAP report if applying for ReCAP. If the previous CAP report cannot be located, contact the CAP staff at cap@heritagepreservation.org. A copy of the report will be mailed to the museum for a fee of $30.

- located in one of the fifty states of the United States of America, the District of Columbia, the Commonwealth of Puerto Rico, Guam, American Samoa, the Virgin Islands, the Commonwealth of the Northern Mariana Islands, the Republic of the Marshall Islands, the Federated States of Micronesia, or the Republic of Palau;
- a museum that, using a professional staff, (1) is organized on a permanent basis for essentially educational or aesthetic purposes; (2) owns or uses tangible objects, either animate or inanimate; (3) cares for these objects; and (4) exhibits these objects to the general public on a regular basis through facilities that it owns or operates.

Any type of museum may participate in CAP, including art, history, children's, natural history, science, and tribal museums, arboreta and botanical gardens, zoos, and aquaria. If a zoo or aquarium is accredited by the Association of Zoos and Aquaria (AZA), it may only apply to have its nonliving collections assessed.[6] CAP is designed for small to midsized museums whose collections and buildings can be adequately assessed within the two-day time limit of the site visit. For museums with collections too large to be assessed in two days, a general conservation survey may be obtained through an IMLS Conservation Project Support grant.[7]

A museum that had a CAP assessment seven or more years ago may be eligible to receive a second CAP assessment through ReCAP. Like the first assessment, the ReCAP consists of a survey of the museum's entire collection and all its facilities and results in a report with prioritized recommendations for improving long-term preservation. If the museum's collection and number of buildings have grown since the first assessment to a size that cannot be assessed within the two-day time limit of the program, the museum may be ineligible for ReCAP. However, Conservation Project Support grants through IMLS or Preservation Assistance Grants through the National Endowment for the Humanities can fund general assessments of collections that have grown too large for CAP.

Before the Site Visit

The museum has two main responsibilities before the site visit. The first is selecting an assessor.[8] The CAP staff at Heritage Preservation matches each participant museum with four conservators (or zoologists or horticulturalists, if applicable) and four historic structure assessors if the museum is housed in a historic building. The participants may review the potential assessors' resumes and choose from that group; they may also consult the list (provided by Heritage Preservation) of all approved CAP assessors in their region or suggest a conservator, zoologist, horticulturalist, or historic preservationist to perform the assessment. Heritage Preservation will contact any proposed assessors to instruct them to apply to become CAP assessors. Only professionals officially approved as CAP assessors may perform CAP assessments.

Whether a museum is contracting with an assessor whose name was provided by Heritage Preservation or with a proposed CAP assessor, it is important to review the assessor's qualifications thoroughly. Although all approved CAP assessors are experienced in performing general assessments, assessors' specialties differ, and the training and background of one assessor may prove more appropriate for the assessment than those of another. For instance, a museum with a significant textile collection may benefit most from an assessment performed by an assessor whose background is in textiles. In addition to reviewing the assessors' resumes, it is imperative to check their references before finalizing a contract. Contact museums the assessor has previously assessed for CAP. These references are provided as part of the assessor information packages supplied by Heritage Preservation. Ask the museum's contact person whether the assessor submitted the report on time, whether he or she was easy to work with and productive on-site, and whether any problems came up during or after the assessment and how the assessor resolved them. Checking references before contracting with an assessor can help avoid problems and delays at the end of the CAP process.

CAP participants negotiate fees for the assessment directly with the assessor. Heritage Preservation does not set fees for assessor professional services; each assessor sets his or her own fees. Once an assessor is selected, both the assessor and the museum's representative sign an agreement (or contract) for the CAP assessment outlining all professional, travel, per diem, and miscellaneous fees for the assessment.[9]

The museum's other pre-assessment obligation is to complete the site questionnaire. This questionnaire is an in-depth survey of all the preventive conservation policies and procedures currently in practice at the institution. It is best to devote a few hours to the completion of the questionnaire in order to provide the assessor with the most accurate picture possible of the museum's conservation practices. Items to have on hand while completing the questionnaire include a list of all staff members with their responsibilities, a list of all current collections-related and institutional policies, procedures, and plans, and a list of each building maintained by the museum along with maintenance plans and records for those buildings.

The Site Visit

The on-site assessment consists of three core components: an entrance interview, a walk-through, and an exit interview. The entrance interview is a chance for the assessor to meet staff members and volunteers whose work directly affects the collections, as well as board members. Board members to include in the entrance interview include the president, members of the collections and facilities committees, and any other board members who have expressed an interest in collections and building conservation. Goals for the assessment should be confirmed among all parties at this point, and the agenda for the visit should be reviewed.

After the entrance interview, the assessor conducts a walk-through of the site, guided by museum staff and board members who are prepared to provide explanations and answer any questions about what the assessor sees. The site visit is guided by the goals the museum's representative and the assessor established in planning the assessment, but it also adheres to the guidelines of topics to be addressed in CAP reports, as outlined in the CAP *Handbook for Assessors*.[10] The assessor examines everything inside and outside the buildings: exhibits, storage areas, work spaces, mechanical or equipment rooms, and grounds. Collections assessors do not conduct a detailed examination of every object in the collection but rather examine the types of collections held by the museum and the conditions under which they are stored and exhibited. The collections assessor reviews policies regarding collections management, handling, security, exhibition, pest management, and emergency preparedness. The assessor examines environmental control practices at the museum, either commenting on systems already in place or suggesting new techniques to monitor the environment, such as the use of light meters and data loggers. The historic structure assessor inspects all museum buildings and reviews all building plans, maintenance logs, and renovation records.

In the exit interview, the assessor may give the museum's staff a preview of the issues that will be covered in the report. The assessor and staff may discuss the conservation concerns identified in the walk-through and how they will be addressed in the report. Preferences for report presentation and organization may also be discussed at this time.

See textbox 1.5 for an example of effective planning by museum staff for a productive site visit.

After the Site Visit

Within two months of the site visit, the assessor submits a draft of the assessment report to the museum. All CAP reports may be reviewed in the draft stage before the final report is submitted to ensure that all information is accurate. During a report review, museum staff often find it necessary to correct various facts and dates. In some cases, museum staff may need to correct information in the report if their responses to the assessor's questions on-site were misunderstood or misinterpreted. In other cases, elaboration on how to implement recommendations or technical information on preventive conservation methods is needed. After the assessor delivers the finished report to the museum, a copy is forwarded to Heritage Preservation, and the assessor's professional fees and travel expenses are paid.

After CAP

Once the assessor's report has been submitted, his or her work has ended, but the museum's work has just begun. Using the CAP report, museum staff can focus on the institution's short-, medium-, and long-range conservation goals, ideally solidifying them in a conservation plan. The conservation plan may be part of a larger institutional long-range plan. No matter how the plan is framed, it is important that it become a plan of action for the institution rather than a document gathering dust on a shelf.

TEXTBOX 1.5

PROFILES IN PRESERVATION: PLANNING FOR A PRODUCTIVE CAP SITE VISIT

Wrightsville Beach Museum of History
Madeline Flagler, executive director of the Wrightsville Beach Museum of History in Wrightsville Beach, North Carolina, outlines the steps she took to ensure that the museum's staff and board were prepared to make their CAP site visit productive and educational:

> Educating the board about the importance of collections conservation and building preservation were important goals for the Wrightsville Beach Museum of History's CAP assessment. I expressed this goal to both our collections and building assessors, who both pledged to answer the board's questions and to provide any additional context necessary to their report recommendations.
>
> A few weeks before the site visit, I emailed the board links to readings on collections stewardship and historic preservation. I sent them guidelines for conservation and historic structure assessments from the websites of Heritage Preservation and the National Trust for Historic Preservation. I also spoke with the local state historic preservation officer to get suggestions for historic preservation readings.
>
> By becoming educated about conservation and historic preservation, the board increased their level of excitement and anticipation for the site visit. By the time the visit was concluded, not only were the staff and board better informed of best practices for stewardship of the collections and historic house, but we understood the concept of conservation priorities well enough to immediately address some of the assessors' preliminary recommendations: for example, the photograph collections were immediately moved to a safer storage area, and the roof was promptly checked for shingles that blew off over the past season.
>
> Because we were prepared for our assessment, the Wrightsville Beach Museum of History's staff and board worked well with our CAP assessors, and we were able to begin implementation of their recommendations with purpose rather than with trepidation. As one of the board members observed of the assessment, "This is not as overwhelming as I thought it would be."

The recommendations in the CAP report can often be divided into two categories: those requiring person power to implement and those requiring funding. Plan and policy writing often fall under the category of person power. By reading reference material about or attending workshops on conservation, long-range, disaster and emergency, and pest management planning, staff can implement recommendations to develop or improve the institution's plans relatively quickly. Museums should celebrate these achievements and ensure that the board is aware of the staff's accomplishments.

The CAP recommendations requiring person-power may necessitate the museum's recruiting additional workers, which often poses a challenge to smaller institutions with low budgets. However, keep in mind that the recommendations sometimes take a few years to achieve, and staff and volunteers can be recruited to join the museum over time. For an example of CAP recommendations leading to projects that increased staff, see textbox 1.6. In addition, in their search for collections employees, many small museums benefit from widening their scope to include temporary workers and interns from local colleges. For guidance on recruiting interns to carry out CAP report recommendations, see textbox 1.7.

TEXTBOX 1.6

PROFILES IN PRESERVATION: CAP REPORT RECOMMENDATIONS AND INSTITUTIONAL GOALS

Stenton Museum
Laura Keim, curator of the Stenton Museum in Philadelphia, Pennsylvania, outlines how implementation of a CAP report recommendation resulted in professional cataloging of the museum's entire collection and the creation of the curator position:

> Stenton has been administered as a museum by the National Society of the Colonial Dames of America in the Commonwealth of Pennsylvania since 1899. The first professional director (and, at the time, only staff member) took the site through the CAP process in 1997. One of the CAP report recommendations was to achieve greater control over the collections, specifically by cataloging them into a database. The director sought funding from the William Penn Foundation, a charitable organization serving the Greater Philadelphia region, for a project to address this need. Stenton received funding from William Penn to hire me as collections consultant and cataloging specialist. We used PastPerfect, and I computerized all the existing collections records, augmented the catalog, and researched other objects related to the site in other institutional and private collections, creating records for them as well. The William Penn Foundation mandated that Stenton then hire a staff person who would be dedicated to the collections, and I was able to stay on as Stenton's first curator. So, as a result of the CAP assessment and a need it flagged, collections maintenance and interpretation are now permanently funded as part of Stenton's operating budget.

PROFILES IN PRESERVATION: RECRUITING INTERNS TO IMPLEMENT CAP REPORT RECOMMENDATIONS

General Lew Wallace Study & Museum
Amanda Wesselmann, associate director of the General Lew Wallace Study
& Museum in Crawfordsville, Indiana, shares her tips on recruiting college
interns to implement CAP report recommendations:

> Much of the work on collections at the General Lew Wallace Study & Museum
> has been completed as projects for temporary collections staff and interns. In-
> tern projects in particular enable the museum to strengthen its relationship with
> area colleges and train the next generation of museum professionals. Projects
> have included rehousing collections in appropriate containers in a designated
> storage facility and reconciling paper and digital records to gain intellectual
> control of the collection.
>
> Developing relationships with your city or state's university faculty members
> in the applied history or museum studies departments is a great way to get your
> internship advertisements to interested students who will have the appropriate
> training and background for museum work. If your institution does not have the
> funds to pay college interns, you can structure the internship in such a way that
> the student can earn college credit for it. With a bit of research, you can find out
> which museum studies and applied history programs incorporate internships for
> credit and how you can design the internship to meet the credit requirements.

Preventive conservation projects and improvements often require outside funding. Small grants for archival rehousing materials are available from federal, state, municipal, and local sources. In addition, keep in mind that a few small museums in the same region can often pool their resources to buy archival materials from national suppliers at a cheaper rate. Cooperative museum projects of this type are often attractive to funders. In order to raise interest and a sense of investment in the care and preservation of collections, it is of paramount importance to inform stakeholders and the community of all conservation initiatives the museum has achieved and grants it has earned.

After a museum obtains local and smaller state grants, application for larger state and federal grants is often the next step in implementing conservation improvements. For an example of how to use the CAP report as a supporting document for further grant applications, see textbox 1.8. For an example of how to use CAP report recommendations to secure dedicated funding for special projects, see textbox 1.9.

TEXTBOX 1.8

PROFILES IN PRESERVATION: CAP, PRESERVATION PLANS, AND FURTHER GRANTS

Logan Museum of Anthropology

Nicolette Meister, curator of collections of the Logan Museum of Anthropology at Beloit College in Beloit, Wisconsin, confirms how the CAP assessment set her museum on the road to further federal grants and even AAM accreditation:

In 2002, the Logan developed a new strategic plan that identified collections improvements as a key goal. The first crucial step was obtaining a CAP survey. The CAP allocation enabled the Logan Museum to consult with an architect and an objects conservator familiar with anthropological collections to assess the current condition of collections and to help prioritize collection needs. The CAP report served as a springboard to launch the museum into preservation planning and grant proposal writing to address the recommendations. The report became the foundation of our preservation plan, which was then used as a supporting document in federal grant proposals. In 2005 the Logan Museum applied for a National Endowment for the Humanities (NEH) Grant for Stabilizing Humanities Collections to upgrade the preservation of and access to the museum's anthropological collection. The key to our success in obtaining this competitive grant was the proposal's grounding in a comprehensive needs assessment and a preservation plan charting a course of action to meet those needs. From 2006 to 2008, the Logan Museum implemented the NEH-funded project and renovated storage areas with new cabinets and compactor storage and rehoused collections in archival materials and mounts.

In addition, the CAP report recommended that the museum consider purchasing data loggers so environmental data could be stored electronically and easily accessed. Using this recommendation, in 2010 the museum applied for an IMLS American Heritage Preservation Grant to purchase data loggers and present a workshop on environmental monitoring to the staff and students in the college's museum studies program. Since 2002, the museum has subscribed to a program of incremental improvements, resulting in an increase in our ability to care for and provide access to over 350,000 ethnographic and archaeological objects, none of which would have been possible without the CAP report.

After years of concerted efforts to improve collections care and to achieve other institutional goals, the Logan Museum was awarded accreditation by the AAM in 2007. The AAM Visiting Committee noted our programmatic commitment to improving collections care.

TEXTBOX 1.9

PROFILES IN PRESERVATION: CAP AND CREATIVE FUNDRAISING

Buffalo Bill Museum
Steve Friesen, director of the Buffalo Bill Museum in Denver, Colorado, shares his tip for obtaining funds to implement a CAP report recommendation:

> Achieving conservation objectives can require patience and persistence. Not everything can be done at once, but over time great things can be achieved. One of my first acts upon becoming director of the Buffalo Bill Museum and Grave in 1995 was to apply for CAP. The CAP report directed our attention to the need to conserve the museum's collection of Wild West posters by naming the project as a top priority. Lacking the funds to restore a large group of the posters at one time, the museum has solicited special donations to conserve an average of one poster each year since the CAP survey. Today, around fifteen posters have been conserved, several of which are prominently exhibited. Recently a special donation was received to conserve five more posters in 2010. The museum's poster-restoration project will be the subject of a special exhibit opening in 2011.

Learn More about CAP

The Conservation Assessment Program is one of many assessment programs that benefit museums by helping to outline and prioritize goals for achieving best practices. There are also the Museum Assessment Program (see page 17) and the Standards and Excellence Program for History Organizations (see page 2). Preservation Assistance Grants, offered by the National Endowment for the Humanities, and Conservation Project Support grants, offered by IMLS, can fund both general and specialized assessments, as well as other projects. CAP is unique in that it is the only federally subsidized assessment program specifically designed for small to midsized institutions to provide preventive conservation advice from a trained conservation professional. The CAP assessment model has proven productive and beneficial for assessors and museums alike. By serving 2,591 museums over the past twenty years, CAP has inspired twenty years' worth of effort and achievement among the stewards of America's collections. For more information, call the CAP office at 202-233-0800 or e-mail cap@heritagepreservation.org.

Resource List

Agencies and Organizations for Grants and Nonprofit Assistance

American Association of Museums: www.aam-us.org

American Association for State and Local History: www.aaslh.org

BoardSource (a nonprofit organization dedicated to advancing the public good by building exceptional nonprofit boards and inspiring board service): www.boardsource.org

Heritage Preservation: www.heritagepreservation.org

Institute of Museum and Library Services: www.imls.gov

Museum Trustee Association (a nonprofit organization dedicated to providing ongoing
board education programs, services, and resources for the special needs of museum
trustees): www.mta-hq.org

National Endowment for the Humanities: www.neh.gov

National Park Service: www.nps.gov

Grants and Technical Assistance Programs

Conservation Assessment Program: www.heritagepreservation.org/CAP

Conservation Project Support, Museums for America, Save America's Treasures, and
American Heritage Preservation Grants: www.imls.gov

Museum Assessment Program: www.aam-us.org/museumresources/map/index.cfm

Preservation Assistance Grants: www.neh.gov

Standards and Excellence Program for History Organizations: www.aaslh.org/steps.htm

Notes

1. The total number of accredited museums on January 1, 2010, was 779.

2. The Heritage Health Index study defined small museums as those with an annual
budget of less than $500,000 per year.

3. American Association of Museums (AAM), *Collections Management, Collections
Maintenance, and Conservation* (Washington, DC: AAM, 1985). The survey, begun in
February 1984 and concluded in June 1985, was conducted by the AAM in cooperation
with the National Institute for the Conservation of Cultural Property (now Heritage
Preservation) and the American Institute for Conservation under contract to the Insti-
tute of Museum Services (now the Institute of Museum and Library Services).

4. See "Conservation Assessment Program Assessor Information," Heritage Preservation, www.heritagepreservation.org/CAP/Assessors.html, for a list of the documentation
submitted by CAP assessors.

5. See the Heritage Preservation website at www.heritagepreservation.org.

6. AZA-accredited institutions will not find CAP useful for living animal collections
because the accreditation survey process is more exhaustive than a CAP survey.

7. For more information, see "Conservation Project Support," IMLS, www.imls.gov/
applicants/grants/conservProject.shtm.

8. "Assessor" will be used in the singular throughout this section, although participating museums often have two assessors.

9. For a copy of the CAP Sample Agreement, see "Information and Resources for
Current CAP Participants," Heritage Preservation, www.heritagepreservation.org/cap/
current.html.

10. See Heritage Preservation, "Conservation Assessment Program Assessor Information."

MAKING A CASE FOR SMALL MUSEUMS
Steve Friesen

Whenever I am in the Napa Valley, I visit my favorite winery. As I drive through the valley, I admire all of the large, well-known wineries with their broad impressive gateways and interesting architecture. Tour buses fill their parking lots, and tourists photograph themselves in front of the buildings. Finally, I turn onto a gravel lane and drive through a vineyard to an unimpressive metal building. When I walk in the door, I see wine barrels stacked from floor to ceiling. In front of me is the tasting area—several upended wine barrels with polished wooden planks laid across them. It is the beginning of a deeply personalized experience, with conversations about weather and wine, food and fashion. The members of the small staff at the winery enjoy their craft, and it shows, even though they are probably not paid as well as the staffs at the larger wineries. Sometimes the owner is wandering about taking care of business and stops to chat. Unlike larger wineries, this place usually produces only six different wines a year. But those often take top prizes in wine competitions, beating out much larger wineries. As a consumer, I am also pleased because the prices are reasonable, and there is no charge for tasting. While I enjoy visiting the large wineries on occasion, I truly enjoy the Napa Valley experience here.

That is the way the ideal small museum can and should operate. It is personalized to the visitor and provides an accessible experience. The building may not be impressive, but the collections are. The exhibits are limited, but they are good. The staff is often underpaid in comparison to larger museums, but theirs is a labor of love. Visitation numbers are not necessarily high, but the constituencies are loyal.

A small museum is not an institution that has not yet grown up to become a big museum. In many, perhaps most, cases, its size is just right. While a small museum can become larger, that is not a prerequisite for or measure of its success.

> A small museum is *not* an institution that has not yet grown up to become a big museum.

There is a tendency in the museum profession to define small museums by what they do not have rather than by what they do have. To many people, a small museum is one with too little money, too few staff, too small facilities, and even too little knowledge. This negative approach stereotypes the small museum as a place that is somehow incomplete or needs desperately to learn from big museums. But size need not be a limitation and can be an advantage. Like my favorite winery, the small museum can offer a product of equal or superior value to that offered by larger institutions.

In reality, small museums often have access to more opportunities than large museums. Small museums also have strengths not possessed by big museums. In fact, large museums can learn much from small museum practice; it is not just a one-way street, as has often been the case in the past.

Just what is a small museum? Like trying to grab a greased pig, creating a universally applicable and acceptable definition of a small museum is very difficult. When I was director of a museum that had one staff member (myself) and a budget of $50,000, I was appalled to hear directors of museums with budgets over $100,000 refer to their institutions as small museums. They have no idea what it is to be small, I thought to myself. But I suspect they too felt that directors of museums with even larger budgets of $200,000 had no idea what it was like to work at a truly small museum. To some degree, it is a matter of perspective; a museum with a $1 million budget is considerably smaller than one with a $15 million budget.

Such subjectivity, or even an "I'll know it when I see it" approach, is not useful. One must finally define what constitutes a small museum. The Small Museums Committee of the American Association for State and Local History (AASLH) defines a small museum as an institution having a budget of less than $250,000 and "a small staff with multiple responsibilities." The definition goes on to note that "other characteristics such as the physical size of the museum, collections size and scope, etc., may further classify a museum as small."

As indicated above, the primary characteristics used to define a small museum are usually budget and staff size. Those are certainly the most easily applied criteria, but as the last line of the definition suggests, there may be other characteristics of small museums. Before discussing budget and staff size, I would like to address these other variables—usually physical size, collections size and scope, and visitation—which are often applied to defining small museums.

Physical size can vary greatly from museum to museum. In the large museum spectrum, there are institutions like the Museum of Fine Arts in Boston or the Oakland Museum, which occupy large structures. There are also large outdoor complexes like Colonial Williamsburg, with its range of structures of all sizes spread over several square miles, and various state-run systems that often

Photo 2.1.   The Buffalo Bill Museum and Grave complex includes a mountaintop location and spectacular views that are not dependent on budget or staff size.

include a large central structure with smaller satellite sites spread over a large geographic area.

Within the spectrum of what are commonly considered small museums, there is a similar variation in physical size. There are museums in large structures (e.g., former courthouses, railroad roundhouses, and even aircraft hangers) that are small museums nonetheless. They may actually occupy more square footage than museums with much larger budgets and staff sizes. And many small museums sit within significantly greater acreage than large museums.

Let me use my own institution as a case in point. The Buffalo Bill Museum and Grave is part of a sixty-four-acre complex that consists mainly of a natural environment that includes an ecosystem of ponderosa pines and granite rocks, perched on the top of a mountain. The site overlooks Denver to the east and the Continental Divide to the west. Our current museum building has a total of seventy-seven hundred square feet, within which we have not only all visitor services but also a gift shop, exhibit areas, and a combination storage/office area. The former museum building, a two-story structure with a footprint of another thirty-five hundred square feet, acts as gift shop, snack bar, and lodging for gift shop employees, who also help provide nighttime security. It is the largest museum gift shop in the Denver metro area. We have extensive picnic facilities and a parking lot that will accommodate over 125 cars. It is a big complex, but if one applies the criteria of budget and staff size, our institution is still a small museum.

I emphasize our physical surroundings and other appurtenances because, if you take them into account, small museums often have large physical facilities, particularly if they are in a rural area. Another example would be the 1719 Hans Herr House near Lancaster, Pennsylvania. When I was director there in the 1980s, the museum had one and a half paid staff members, around twenty-five volunteers, and a very small annual budget. But it was situated on sixteen acres that included barns, outbuildings, and an orchard of heirloom apple trees. The museum included not just the 1719 house but all that land as well, with exhibits of farm machinery in the outbuildings and a small welcome center with offices.

The Buffalo Bill Museum and Grave and the 1719 Hans Herr House are typical of historic houses or sites that occupy an amount of space disproportionate to their budget. These small museums are frequently larger, in terms of physical space occupied, than many museums that would be considered large based on their budget and staff.

The AASLH definition also refers to collection size and scope. As our understanding of what comprises a museum has expanded over the last fifty years, collections have become less critical to determining what truly is a museum. One result of this change is that the size of a museum's collection is not as important as it once was. Indeed, some museums in today's world have no collections at

Photo 2.2. The nearly three-hundred-year-old farmstead complex surrounding the 1719 Hans Herr House provides a wide range of scenic and interpretive opportunities.

all, choosing to mount exhibitions of borrowed materials only. Thus, it is very possible for an institution to have a very large budget, staff, and building, yet have few, if any, collection items. On the other hand, a local historical society, run entirely by volunteers and with a small budget, might have several thousand artifacts in its collection. Despite its larger collections size, the local historical society is, nonetheless, a small museum.

Similarly, the scope of collections varies greatly across different museum sizes. Compare what is probably the largest collection of saddles in the world at the Don King Museum in Sheridan, Wyoming, with one of the largest collections of timepieces at the National Watch and Clock Museum in Columbia, Pennsylvania. Each has a comparatively narrow scope, but the former is housed in a small building with a very small staff, while the latter has a large building with a large staff. Similarly, railroad museums have a narrow scope of collecting, but they range in size from very small to very large institutions. Collections scope, like size, simply cannot be used to define a small museum.

Visitation has sometimes been used as a unit of measurement to distinguish the small museum from larger institutions. Yet visitation, like physical size, is not consistent with institutional size. The Buffalo Bill Museum and Grave site, with its sixty-five acres, attracts close to half a million visitors annually. They visit the gift shop, read interpretive signs around the site, see the grave, have a picnic, and enjoy the mountain environment. Those who visit the museum building itself number around sixty thousand each year (because an admission fee is charged). But the museum has oversight of the entire site and provides services to all visitors in one form or another. Nevertheless, according to the criteria of budget and staff size, the Buffalo Bill Museum and Grave is a small museum.

We are not alone in being a small museum facility that serves large numbers of visitors. If you look at the visitation at the Paul Revere House in Boston and the Betsy Ross House in Philadelphia, you will find around two hundred thousand visitors crowding their fairly small buildings every year. Many places that would be considered large museums would love to attract that sort of attendance.

So, do the characteristics of physical size, collections, and visitation apply to defining the small museum? I do not think so. As I have already pointed out, there are too many variables within those characteristics. As suggested earlier, staff size and budget are still the best objective criteria to apply in defining the small museum.

So which staff and budget sizes define small museums? The AASLH definition supplied earlier establishes a budget of $250,000 and a "small staff" as its criteria. According to the Institute of Museum and Library Services (IMLS), a small museum has a full-time staff of five or fewer and/or a budget of less than $250,000. The American Association of Museums (AAM) considers a small museum to be an institution with a full-time staff of five or fewer and a budget of $350,000 or less. Synthesizing the criteria established by AASLH, IMLS, and AAM, one can conclude that a small museum has a paid staff of five or fewer persons and a budget of no more than $350,000. Those criteria apply to the Buffalo Bill Museum and Grave, the 1719 Hans Herr House, and the other small museums I have discussed this far.

But there is so much more to small museums than a measurement of quantity or statistics. Returning to my favorite winery, I like it not just because it is small but because of what its smallness enables it to do. I like it because of the more intimate experience it offers. The same applies to museums.

So, let us look beyond such quantitative characteristics as budgets or staff size when we assess the small museum. The more qualitative characteristics of small museums must be considered. For this purpose, I will use a definition of qualitative as having the "training, skill, or ability for a special purpose."

> More resources enable quality but don't guarantee it.

A big problem with applying only numerical criteria, such as budget or staff size, to small museums is the unspoken message that they are somehow less or inadequate. Many people have the idea that "small" is not confined just to size but also describes quality or ability. We have all heard the term *small museum* used as a negative judgment, not just as a description: "I guess that's the way things are done in small museums." "A small museum just couldn't handle that." "I'm surprised that a small museum was able to do that program." Such statements imply that small museums are somehow sloppier, not up to standards, or simply not able to do the job that is done by big museums.

A variety of assumptions accompany these mistaken ideas. When it comes to staff, there is the belief that big museums can afford to pay for the best. This assumption implies that those who work in small museums are less than the cream of the crop. When it comes to collections, the best collections are at those museums that can afford to acquire them—in other words, the big museums. When it comes to exhibits, big museums put on the blockbusters that everyone wants to see, whereas small museum exhibits are forgettable. When it comes to trends, big museums set the pace in our field, and small museums simply follow their lead. These, however, are all mistaken assumptions

I will admit that some of them hold a bit of truth. Big museums can hire more staff and pay higher salaries. They can send staff for training at conferences and meetings. They can allow staff to take on leadership roles in the museum community. They can pay for fancier graphics and electronics, hire better-known entertainers for programs, and attract more donations. But as tempting as it might be to do so, we cannot assume that large budgets and staffs equal better museums. More resources enable quality but do not guarantee it.

Big museums do not necessarily have better staffs because of their budgets. They do not necessarily have better programs or exhibits because of their budgets; nor are they more innovative because of their larger staffs. I have been to some very expensive and simply awful exhibits at big museums. And I have to question the wisdom of some of the trends in our field that have been driven by big museums, such as overreliance on electronics for interpretation and the establishment of exorbitant use fees for photographic reproductions.

But I am not here to criticize big museums; I am here to praise and encourage small ones. There are wonderful large museums, but there are many wonderful small museums. The point is that just as more resources do not ensure quality, fewer resources, particularly financial, do not guarantee that a museum will have less quality.

Quality is not numerically based. Take, for example, music. A judgement of musical excellence is not based upon the number of performers but upon intrinsic standards associated with a particular type of performance. Thus, there are large performing groups like orchestras, marching bands, and big bands. But there are also small jazz combos, quartets, solo performers, and so forth. While some people may prefer an orchestral performance to one by a string quartet, no one assumes that a string quartet is less proficient because of its size. Size does not matter in evaluating musical quality or impact. After all, a quartet of four lads from Liverpool revolutionized the music world. In fact, rock and roll had its origins in small groups. Just as no one looks at size to evaluate the quality of music or the potential of musical groups, the same orientation should exist for museums.

Some musicians prefer to perform in a small group; I have chosen to work in small history museums during my career. I have worked in these museums for over thirty years because I like them. One of the things I like is that there is a lot of freedom in small museums. For one thing, the committee meetings are smaller and fewer. When we make staff decisions, we do not deal with twenty-five opinions; we deal with five. Small museums have a lot more flexibility and can move much more rapidly as a result. After all, small boats are easier to turn than big boats.

If small museums lack anything, it is the big ego that is necessary to transcend the hurdles that encourage small thinking. Usually all that prevents small museums from thinking big are self-imposed limits. But small museums can and should think big.

It's not the size of the dog in the fight; it's the size of the fight in the dog.

During childhood, we are given examples of small being successful, even prevailing over the large. Our childhood stories range from "The Little Engine That Could" to the biblical account of David and Goliath. But as we get older, we often forget these lessons and need to be reminded of the power in being small. A favorite event of mine at the annual National Western Stock Show in Denver is the dog pull. It is not the St. Bernards or Great Danes that pull the heaviest weights; they usually are not even in the competition because their large body structures cannot handle weight pulling. It is the small breeds that are impressive, often pulling weights ten times their own size. Those dogs may be physically small, but in their own minds, they are huge. This brings to mind an old saying, repeated by everyone from Mark Twain to Dwight D. Eisenhower: "It's not the size of the dog in the fight; it's the size of the fight in the dog."

In *Starting Right: A Basic Guide to Museum Planning*, Gerald George and Cindy Sherrell-Leo, both staunch small museum advocates, give the following advice to people thinking about starting a museum: "Your museum is not going to have to be *huge* to be *good*. Unless your resources are extraordinary, you are not going to create a new Louvre or Smithsonian Institution—nothing on such a grand scale as that is required, or even necessarily desirable, for a museum to serve its community splendidly well."

All of us who work in small museums need to hear this advice on a regular basis. It is particularly important to hear after we have undertaken our own busman's holiday, visiting some of the big museums we have always heard about, or been bedazzled by presentations by large museums at professional meetings. The fact that there are magnificent large museums out there does not mean that we should aspire to be them or to even be like them. There are also magnificent small museums that do not aspire to be big museums and serve their communities every bit as well as large museums.

In fact, most small museums enjoy close relationships with their communities, as suggested by George and Sherrell-Leo. Small museums participate in such communitywide events as parades and festivals, even farmer's markets. Museum staff members are often active in civic organizations and local politics. These relationships pay off; community volunteer groups provide small museums with everything from gardening to research, as well as serving as docents, gift shop clerks, and donors.

Photo 2.3. The most prominent natural and historical landmark of Gillette, Wyoming, provides the name for the museum that preserves and interprets its heritage.

Because of their size, small museums fill very important niches, often serving very diverse communities. There are local history museums that preserve and interpret the history of the town or county within which they reside. A good example would be the Rockpile Museum in Gillette, Wyoming, named after a large pile of rocks in the middle of town. Situated near this geological formation, which settlers used as a landmark, the museum collects and interprets the history of the community. There are many museums that preserve and share the story of a particular religious or ethnic group, like the Kauffman Museum in North Newton, Kansas, which tells the story of the Mennonites who settled the area. Some small museums maintain both community history and ethnic culture, like the myriad of small Pennsylvania German museums in Lancaster, Berks, Montgomery, and Bucks counties. There are small museums that concentrate on a particular subject area, such as firefighting, quilt, carousel, and railroad museums. Some small museums may have very staunch local support as well as a national, even international, constituency. The Colorado Railroad Museum in Golden is a small museum with an active local volunteer base and a national membership. It tells the story of Colorado railroading, but that subject's appeal transcends the museum's locale.

Sometimes a small museum springs up around a single person's vision, creating a collection with a unique perspective. In Denver, Hugh Grant's Kirkland Museum of Fine and Decorative Art exhibits a collection of works by regional artist Vance Kirkland, surrounded by the work of many of his twentieth-century contemporaries. It includes decorative arts items, like Frank Lloyd Wright furniture and Bakelite radios, as well as fine arts. The combination of these somewhat eclectic materials works because they reflect a particular aesthetic during a particular period in American history. Like that of the Colorado Railroad Museum, the Kirkland Museum's community is both local and national because of the institution's unique subject matter.

In these respects, perhaps "small" is a misnomer; borrowing from the world of wines, cheese, and breads, many small museums could be instead regarded as artisanal. They are carefully crafted to meet a particular mission and provide a particular service. They are different from larger museums not so much because of their subject matter but because of how their size enables them to present the subject matter. They are string quartets, not orchestras. And, like my favorite winery, they concentrate on limited production appealing to a certain taste. The difference between one of these small institutions and a state historical society museum, for example, is as great as the difference between an art museum and a science museum.

The small museum has many opportunities and advantages in the twenty-first century. The computer age and the Internet have empowered small museums like never before. When I started my first small museum job back in 1976,

Photo 2.4. The placement of Vance Kirkland's art within the context of furniture contemporary to his period creates a period room with stunning visual and interpretive impact.

I used a large-type manual typewriter to create exhibit labels. For titles I used rub-on transfer letters that were frustrating to position and nearly always looked sloppy. The only other alternative was to have titles and labels produced by a printer, something that was too expensive for my museum. Today, our computers make available to us a nearly infinite variety of fonts and font sizes. We can merge symbols and illustrations with our label copy to make it more interesting, then print the labels on a comparatively inexpensive computer printer. That same printer can be used to print photographs. When we need titles, we can take electronic files to a local quick-print shop and have them made for a fraction of what they would have cost thirty years ago. Even graphics like murals, posters, and banners can be printed commercially for less than in the past.

Computers have also made collections management much easier for small museums. The catalog forms and multiple note cards of the past have given way to a single database entry that is quickly and easily searched. Data entry is much easier and more volunteer friendly than in the past. The smaller collections of many small museums also make conversion to computerized collection databases a much less involved process than for large museums.

Photo 2.5.   Using new printing technologies, images and text can be combined into murals, which are then fronted by artifacts and easily read slopers, with running commentary, as in this exhibit at the Buffalo Bill Museum and Grave.

Computers further enable small museums to more readily share collections than ever before. Not only can collections information be kept and quickly accessed on a computer, but images of artifacts can also be easily and inexpensively made with a digital camera. Even if the computerized database does not allow imbedding or attaching of photos, the assignment of an accession number to both the database file and the photo file makes retrieval of images a quick process. Thus, exhibit planning becomes more efficient, and responses to collections inquiries can be made much more quickly. With the computerized database supplying images and information about artifacts, there is less need to handle them, which improves collections care.

Responding to requests for copies of photographs or documents in a museum's collection is much easier as well. High-resolution digital scans can be easily created and stored for those images most frequently requested. The images can be made available by CD or even as attachments to e-mails when requested. All that is needed is a computer and a reasonably good scanner.

Fulfillment of requests for assistance—whether it be to provide artifact loans to other museums for exhibits or to provide images of collections materials (such as photographs)—is one area in which small museums appear to have a distinct advantage over large museums. The comparatively simple digital processes described above seem to become much more complicated as an institution gets larger. Because of internal bureaucracies at big museums, loans take longer to process and images longer to provide. Small museums have an agility, or at least a potential for agility, in working with collections records that is not duplicated at large museums. A simple request for even a single loan item usually takes months to be processed by a large museum, while a small museum can process it in days, despite having fewer personnel. And when it comes to providing digital images of photographs, most small museums are light years ahead of large museums in prompt and hassle-free fulfillment.

The Internet is a great equalizer, enabling small museums to present the same online profile as large museums. A small museum can market itself just as effectively on the Internet as a large museum because search engines do not consider institutional size. The Internet is a level playing field for museums, no matter their size. A small museum can provide as much and as effective Internet content as a large museum. A museum's website can be limited to largely marketing or it can include extensive information. The volunteer-operated Sharpsteen Museum in Calistoga, California, has a very well-organized and straightforward website aimed at marketing itself and its programs. Another volunteer-run organization, the Ford County Historical Society in Dodge City, Kansas, has a very large Internet site that includes a history of the county, of Dodge City itself, and of other aspects of the Old West. In the case of each of these institutions, the critical factors in creating an aggressive Internet site were vision, initiative, and time.

The fact that a small museum has a smaller budget than a large museum can prevent it from taking advantage of those opportunities offered by the greater funding available to a large museum. In coping with the challenges of operating on a smaller budget, however, a small museum can throw creativity rather than money at problems. That is not to say that large museums are less creative, only that large sums of money do not guarantee creativity any more than they guarantee quality.

This resilience in the face of budgetary challenges works to the advantage of the small museum in difficult times. A budget cut at a small museum could result in the loss of one out of three staff members. A comparable budget cut at a large museum could mean the loss of ten out of thirty employees. Each is equally devastating initially. But it is usually easier for the small museum to find funding to replace that single position than for the larger museum to fill the ten positions. The larger the institution, the more difficult problem solving becomes regarding budget and many other aspects of operations.

Small museums also compensate for lack of budgetary or personnel resources by collaborating. Throughout the country, small museums have banded together

Photo 2.6. Exhibits at the Kauffman Museum were created in collaboration with professors and students at Bethel College, the Mennonite school with which it is affiliated.

into local museum collaboratives, doing everything from sharing resources to marketing jointly. Such collaboratives have reached out to other community nonprofits, ranging from cultural groups like symphonies to churches and colleges. Again, museums of any size can take part in collaborative activities; yet collaboration is often more effective when accomplished by smaller institutions. That effectiveness is due at least in part to the ability of participants to make decisions about projects, unhindered by the internal processes and inertia that often slow decision-making at larger institutions.

Leadership is a critical component in museums of any size. It is particularly important to small museums. A leader, in the form of an executive director or the president of a board in an all-volunteer museum, can have a great deal more impact in a small institution than in a large institution. This can be positive or negative. Bad leadership can quickly undermine a small museum, but, on the other hand, a small museum can soar with good leadership. In fact, a good leader can often have more impact in a small museum. It is much more difficult to "turn the boat" in a large museum precisely because of its size.

Just as small size in terms of staff and budget brings certain advantages, we must acknowledge that it does present challenges. I prefer to approach these challenges as "opporthreats"—situations that can be either opportunities or threats, depending on your approach to them. And there is no shortage of opporthreats facing small museums.

One of the biggest opporthreats faced by all museums, but particularly by small museums, is that of getting visitors to return. "Oh, I don't need to visit; I saw the museum two years ago," is not an uncommon statement in reaction to an invitation to visit a local museum. Large museums have the advantage of providing a much greater breadth of permanent exhibits than small museums, but they also must confront this attitude. That is why many larger museums change temporary exhibits as often as four to six times a year. Small museums must change exhibits as well, even if not as frequently as a large museum. But this can be an opportunity, not a threat.

Small museums should be as ambitious in creating changing exhibits as large museums. Budget and personnel size need not be limiting factors. The two main options for changing exhibits are renting traveling exhibits and creating exhibits in-house. Each has advantages and disadvantages. Renting exhibits saves personnel time but may be more costly than creating exhibits in-house. Creating exhibits in-house enables a small museum to customize them to its audiences and to follow the institutional purpose more closely, but doing so also takes a good deal of time. The small museum will need to decide which option best suits its budgetary and personnel constraints, its audiences, and the stories it wishes to tell. In either case, providing changing exhibits is an opportunity that allows the small museum to strengthen its existing constituencies as well

Photo 2.7. Throughout the year the Colorado Railroad Museum holds very popular "steam-up days," when volunteers power up the rolling stock and provide visitors with rides.

as attract new constituencies. The process of creating new exhibits can further revitalize everything from collections acquisition (when potential donors are inspired by an exhibit to give artifacts) to educational programming (which can be linked to the new exhibits). Changing exhibits are critical to maintaining a vibrant and successful small museum.

Programming is as important to small museums as it is to large museums. This can run a gamut of offerings ranging from special events like festivals and lecture series to educational and family activities. It all depends upon the needs of the museum's constituency and the museum's ability to meet those needs.

For many years, school programs have been at the core of educational offerings from museums of all sizes. Yet the nature of school visits is changing as schools find they have fewer resources. School visits are dropping, and some museums are finding that, in order to continue school programming, they must provide more and more incentives, ranging from offering free programs to actually busing students to the institution. This is an opportunity for small museums, not a threat. Retooling entire educational programs can be very difficult for a large museum, which may have allocated large amounts of funding and personnel to such programs. A small museum can usually respond more rapidly to outside change by adjusting its approach to programs. In the case of the Buffalo Bill Museum and Grave, we have greatly decreased our school offerings and concentrated on programming for family visits. This was initially propelled by a decrease in school visits but has been further justified by new information suggesting that family visits, not school visits, lead to more repeat visitation.

As already mentioned, collecting varies widely from museum to museum, with some institutions doing no collecting at all. For the small museum, collecting can be an opporthreat. Yes, it can create storage challenges, but collecting is an important way of connecting to a museum's constituency. People think of museums as collecting institutions and often support museums financially based upon that assumption. For this reason, a small museum that is considering freezing collections acquisitions, or even becoming a noncollecting institution, needs to assess its constituencies or potential constituencies very carefully. Cutting back on collections acquisition because of diminished collections storage could end up being much more costly than finding a way to expand collections storage. This is not to say that a museum should accept donations of anything and everything, but rather that the choice to accept or not accept donations can impact all aspects of operations. In this area, as in others, the museum must be true to its mission.

> Excellence, success, and quality are achievable by, and should be the goals of, any museum, no matter its size.

Being true to its mission is just one way that a museum can strive for excellence. The museum field has been working on the creation of universally applicable standards and best practices for some time. For over thirty years, the AAM struggled with this project. The effort began with its Accreditation Program, continued through the establishment of its Code of Ethics for Museums, and culminated in the publication of the book *National Standards and Best Practices for U.S. Museums* in 2008. The AASLH adopted an ethics statement in 2002 for institutions engaged in the preservation and interpretation of history. Later, AASLH also began its Standards and Excellence Program for History Organizations.

Just as ethics are not confined to any particular size of museum, national standards and best practices are not dependent upon a museum's size. Attaining established standards and practices is simply part of every museum's journey toward excellence. Excellence, success, and quality are achievable by, and should be the goals of, any museum, no matter its size.

These goals can be enhanced, not hampered, by a small museum's size. Small museums' failure to achieve them as effectively as large museums results not from budget or personnel restrictions but a lack of will. Some small

Photo 2.8.   The Los Alamos Historical Society actively preserves and interprets historical sites associated with the Manhattan Project, including the house of Robert Oppenheimer.

museums accomplish these tasks very effectively, demonstrating resilience and community effectiveness, while others tend to use budget or a lack of personnel as a justification. But this is only an excuse. The Los Alamos Historical Society in New Mexico is run primarily by a part-time staff and, like many such institutions, has comparatively minimal funding. The society is nevertheless very involved with its community, has an engaged board, and employs a dedicated staff. Staff members are active in museum professional organizations and strive toward self, as well as institutional, improvement. Despite dealing with a variety of facility challenges, the society's museum attracts thousands of international visitors as well as locals. Not content to rest on its accomplishments, which are considerable considering its size, the society is ambitious in planning its future. It collaborates with other organizations and asks for professional assistance when needed. It is not alone; small historical societies and museums throughout the country are ambitious and accomplishing a great deal, despite limited financial resources.

Back in 1959, the AASLH issued the first primer for small museums. In his opening to *The Management of Small History Museums*, author Carl E. Guthe wrote that the majority of museums in the United States were small history museums. He also stated, "The character of the entire museum movement is likely to be judged locally by their achievements." Little has changed. Today, the majority of museums in the United States are still small history museums. And the character of the museum movement has indeed been judged by their achievements. Taken together, America's small museums not only attract more visitors than their larger peers but survive so substantially on local support that they are a manifestation of the public's enthusiasm for museums in general.

Like my favorite winery, a small museum is a place where the public has the chance to feel completely engaged, encouraged by an enthusiastic and accessible staff. It is a very personal experience that is unimpaired by budget and often enhanced by staff size. A visitor's question about an exhibit will frequently be answered by the person who installed it, and the director might stop for a chat. In a small museum, excellence is not measured by size but by the ability to provide a meaningful product. Yes, for reporting purposes, we will probably still need to define small museums by such statistics as budget and staff size. But those are just statistics and do not tell the full story. The rest of the story? At its best, a small museum is resilient, quick, and innovative. It is a great place to visit and a great place to work.

MISSION AND VISION AGAIN?
WHAT'S THE BIG DEAL?

Harold Skramstad and Susan Skramstad

Why Are Mission and Vision Statements So Important?

One of the most interesting aspects of working with museums as consultants is finding out what the people who are intimately involved with them, usually the governing authority and staff, consider to be of critical importance to their organization. It goes without saying that we are seldom called to work with a smoothly functioning organization; the services and expertise of consultants are usually sought only after the organization has become aware that something is not right. The question is this: "What is that something?" If the organization itself were able to identify it, it would fix it. But the closer one is to a problem, the harder it is to see it. Backing up a bit and using new eyes often brings a broader, clearer view of the organization as a whole. And talking about it tends to focus attention on what is important.

The day-to-day operational issues are what the people inside the organization have to deal with and therefore what they see. From the perspective of ground zero, it is the way the patient "presents," to use medical jargon, that is the most important matter. The patient's symptoms indicate illness and must be addressed in order to effect a cure. Everything else is theory, and we do not have time for that, do we? In the absence of a strong hand guiding treatment, or the experience of a lifetime directing diagnosis, or agreement among those responsible as to what the problem is and what should be done to address it, the patient, in this case the organization, will probably get worse.

We look at the "patient" somewhat differently. We want to know the cause of the illness. The symptoms, after all, only show that there is a problem and, as the patient's condition worsens, that something must be done. The symptoms are certainly interesting and must eventually be addressed, but they are not the cause and will not lead to the cure. And at this point, we always go back to basics, and to us that means we look at the foundation on which the organization stands. What is the bedrock? What holds, or should hold, the place and the people together? What is sturdy enough to withstand the vicissitudes of time and circumstance? What forces focus? What helps the organization to say no to some things and yes to others? What keeps everyone moving in the same direction?

From our point of view, the answer to each of these questions, and to any other question of a fundamental nature about the organization, is, of course, a return to mission and vision. Many organizations give only a perfunctory nod to the importance of these two fundamental statements. They know they must have them, and they must have a strategic plan as well, but it is so much easier and quicker and more exciting to do what you want to do—and charge forward. No one wants to be slowed down by looking at the fundamentals. There are things to be done and new opportunities to be seized and new directions to try and new ideas to listen to—a perfect recipe for disaster.

The title of this chapter gives away our bias right at the beginning, and we make no apologies for our insistence on the importance of mission and vision. Without a shared understanding of the organization's purpose and the value it gives to its users (mission), as well as what it has directed itself to achieve in the fullness of time (vision)—in our universe that is about ten years—there can be no successful path to the future. Working without mission and vision is like setting out on a road trip—let us say from Boulder, Colorado, where we live, to Nome, Alaska, where we might want to go—without a roadmap. We probably both have some sense of where Nome is—actually only Harold would, and he would be pretty shaky—but beyond that, we would only be wandering. And as we wandered, would we agree on which road to take at critical junctures? Doubtful. Pretty soon we would probably begin to question why we even wanted to go to Nome. Why not just head for Santa Fe, New Mexico? We know where that is.

So will it be in a museum without a statement of mission (developed and ratified by the governing authority and staff) to provide direction. There will be lots of time wasted on taking the wrong road and plenty of infighting; focus will begin to dissolve; there will be no shared sense of purpose and at best an inchoate visitor experience. And speaking of visitors, if we have neither a mission nor a vision—translate that to mean that we have no clear understanding of our unique purpose and value or of what we hope to achieve—how can we appropriately serve our users? Chances are we have never even considered who they are, who they should be, who they will be, and why they would come to our museum in the first place. What do we have that they want? If we have never thought about who they are and what we are uniquely equipped to give them, how can we possibly give them an experience they will value? And why—this is an extremely important question—would they or anyone else want to come to our museum, much less support it?

So, we have to go back to basics. And very few organizations want to go there. There is a surprising lack of understanding about the importance of the basic documents, which form the foundation of our organizations. Some organizations

OUR PERSPECTIVE AS CONSULTANTS

We are museum planning consultants who have worked with a lot of organizations over the past fifteen years. We weren't always consultants. Harold
Skramstad was chief of exhibition programs at the Smithsonian Institution's
National Museum of American History, director of the Chicago Historical
Society, and president of the Henry Ford Museum and Greenfield Village,
now known as the Henry Ford. Susan Skramstad was executive assistant
to the chancellor at the University of Michigan, Dearborn, and then vice
chancellor for institutional advancement at the same institution. The only
reason we mention our background here is to shed some light on the perspective we bring to working with museums. Since we were practitioners in
our fields for a long time before we became consultants, we understand what
organizations go through; we have experienced many of the same challenges
you are facing. We have worked with boards, staffs, donors, communities,
volunteers, political entities, competitors, visitors, educators, schools, the ups
and downs of the economy, and everything else that enters into the mix of
nonprofit work, particularly in the area of museums. So we think we bring to
each museum we work with our years of experience "on the inside," as well
as the fresh eyes of an outsider.

By "coming in cold" to a museum seeking our help, we have a great
advantage over those who are already in the middle of things. We are not
hampered by relationships, or vested interest, or a need to skirt problems in
order to keep our jobs within the museum's hierarchy. We have been asked
for our advice and help, and that's what we give.

Our practice from the beginning has been to ask board and staff members
to communicate with us individually in advance of our first visit to their site
and to tell us what, in their opinion, the three most critical issues facing the
organization are. And so a chorus of voices outlines the problems. Perhaps
their visitation is declining; perhaps they are unable to raise the money
necessary for operation at full potential (and who is these days?). Often
there are problems with the board, or problems with the staff, or problems
with the community. Or maybe it's those pesky visitors, the ones who just
don't "get it" about the museum. And so, we receive and review the lists and
prepare to meet with those in whom is vested responsibility for the health
of the organization. Rarely does mission or vision appear on anyone's list.

think of it as "make-work" and a waste of time. After all, they have important work to do; the museum is foundering; they already have a mission and vision. What is the big deal?

The big deal is that without a focused, well-thought-out, agreed-upon purpose and value statement (mission) and without knowing what you hope to achieve by a specific time (vision), you will not be able to

- make a case for your museum—no matter the size;
- have adequate, effective, efficient governance (leadership);
- even think about strategic planning (to achieve what?);
- plan process and activities (toward what end?);
- honor best practices, in your own unique way, on behalf of your own unique museum.

Once we have initiated a serious conversation about mission and vision, people invariably become interested in the process because, in fact, the process (taking the organization apart piece by piece and then putting it back together again) is often as important as the final product (a clear understanding of the essence of the organization's purpose, value, and work). But we will talk more about that in a minute. Right now, let us look back and see how we got to where we are.

Over the last thirty years or so, the change in museums and historical organizations has been nothing short of cataclysmic. For many years the value of our organizations was thought to be self-evident. Governing authorities, staffs, and stakeholders were the stewards of collections, the importance of which was understood by these stewards and by the people who visited and participated in the life of museums. Many generations of museum and historical organization boards and staffs were brought up on the idea that a museum's purpose was "to collect, preserve and interpret . . . ," and their mission statements invariably began that way. The public, hearing this justification over and over, accepted it and thought of museums as important places, quiet places, contemplative places, places for the initiated, the sophisticated, the upwardly mobile, the educated, the elite. So it was a time of "ins" and "outs," and both, with relatively little trauma, accepted their place. The "ins" came to museums; the "outs" did not bother because there was nothing there for them anyway. Many of you will remember those somewhat simpler days. Some of you may still be living in them, may still have a mission that justifies your museum's continued existence by the fact that it collects, preserves, and interprets.

Do not misunderstand. We are not saying there is anything wrong with collections or collecting or with preservation or interpretation. Quite the contrary. But we see these activities as tools toward mission, as the means, not the end.

Many, but not all, museums have collections of true historical and/or associational importance, and some of these museums use their collections well. We say some because using your collection well, and even the act and art of collecting for your museum, depends upon a clear understanding of the museum's mission in the world as well as its aspirations for the future. Mission. Vision.

For young people entering the museum and historical organization field today, it is difficult to comprehend just how much our organizations have changed in the last several decades. We will mention four of these changes, the four that we feel have transformed the field the most:

- *Audience:* This is the most obvious. Museums and historical organizations now serve a much more pluralistic and diverse audience rather that just the few who already have an interest in history. The result, of course, is a great increase in the number of users and a much wider diversity of their expectations.
- *Boundaries:* The distinctions that are so important to museum and historical organization professionals are irrelevant to our users. Profit making versus nonprofit, museum versus library, history museum versus children's museum—whatever it is, they do not care. If we look around, we see Las Vegas gambling casinos with major art collections and exhibitions; a significant historical collection of rock and roll materials developed by the Hard Rock Café chain, professionally curated and conserved; and ownership of a major aquarium in Denver (which failed as a nonprofit) transferred to a restaurant that, while keeping an aquarium-style visitor experience, uses the main tank as the backdrop for its dining room. People use and affiliate with organizations that give them value.
- *Programming:* Increasingly the success of the museum or historical organization is less dependent on the importance of its collections, including historic sites, than on the imagination and programming skills of its staff. In fact, many of the most successful museums today, such as children's museums, art centers, and science and technology centers, may not have collections at all.
- *Mission-driven orientation:* For several generations, a relentless drive toward professionalization among museum and historical-organization practitioners resulted in higher standards in everything from collection preservation and documentation to the production values of exhibitions and the quality of research and programming. The increasing pluralism of museum and historical organization audiences has resulted in new and often contradictory pressures on organizations, which clearly could not be addressed by professional-

ization and the raising of operational standards. It was obvious that something else would have to be developed, or redeveloped, in order to adequately address the multiplicity of new demands being made of every organization. In the last several decades, museums and historical organizations have moved inexorably from being professionally driven to being mission driven.

And no one should have been surprised. From the beginning of our history, museums and historical organizations have been rooted in community. Like libraries, colleges and universities, and other cultural organizations, they have been essential building blocks of the community. In his wonderful 1939 study, *The Museum in America*, Laurence Vail Coleman writes, "The Museum, like the library, is a community enterprise in its very nature."

In our society, communities are not static but fluid and ever changing. People come and go, populations become more diverse, and there are increasing numbers of organizations and institutions they can use or affiliate with. As communities grow, change, and develop, people living within the loose association of geographical boundaries of the community become more vocal about their needs. And we in the museum and historical organization field are bombarded by often contradictory—and sometimes unreasonable—expectations from our communities. How can we as organizations navigate in constantly changing times and with constantly changing communities, keeping in mind that, in the end, our communities, our audiences, may not be restricted by geography at all but rather by interest, or in the case of the ubiquitous tourist, by the general desire to learn about things, or in the case of the school child and education community, by curriculum requirements and standardized testing. Such a navigation system cannot depend on professional standards or best practices mandated or sanctioned by professional or industrywide associations; it must depend instead on special and distinctive qualities, unique to each individual organization.

Almost twenty years ago, Harold wrote in the January–February 1993 issue of *Museum News*,

> The word "museum" has lost its power to adequately define a coherent body of institutions that have similar missions, goals, and strategies. To define a major research-driven natural history museum, a regional science and technology center, an encyclopedic art museum, and a local volunteer-run historical society as a "museum" is like describing General Motors, Kmart, a regional bank, and a local convenience store as a "business"—accurate but not helpful.
>
> In the world of the future, every individual institution, including museums, must be judged on its distinctive ability to provide value to society in a way that builds on unique institutional strengths and serves unique community needs.

The only rule that will apply to all museums is that there are no rules that apply to all museums (with the exception of the most basic and technical rules for keeping track of money and collections). The high ground of object-centered transcendence, of a canon of authoritative knowledge, of codified and concise professional standards to train and guide all museum operations, has lost its power to shape and control.

If this observation is correct, it means that each individual museum or historical organization is going to have to make its own distinctive way in the world.

We suggest that the best gyroscope for setting the distinctive course of any organization is a clear mission. A good mission establishes the distinctiveness and importance of what the organization does and its value to the communities it serves. In the world of the twenty-first century, the key question being asked of every organization is this: "What is the value proposition?" A good mission statement is the answer to that question.

It is here that the traditional mission statement, "to collect, preserve, and interpret . . . ," fails. If we can no longer assume that such activities are an intrinsic good understood and valued by all, and it is clear that we cannot, we must look closely to mission to see how it can help us to organize, focus, and deliver in our own unique way. In arriving at a mission statement for our organizations today, we must ask two fundamental questions: "So what?" and "Who cares?" These short questions may sound like taunts from a schoolyard, but the answers are critical to our success. In developing a mission statement, we must address the fundamental value added of our organization.

Developing a Mission Statement

Experience has confirmed our essential belief that the words in the organizational mission statement are probably the most important words an organization will ever write. Not only are the *words* important, but the *process* by which the organization arrives at those words is central to its success, to the achievement of good and appropriate governance, to the ability to write, understand, and carry out a strategic plan, to the ability to serve its audiences, and to carving out for itself a unique place in the world. Organizations must make themselves important to people outside their walls, so important that they would be very much missed if they were not there, so important that their not being there is unthinkable. If an organization is able to achieve that, it will surely have achieved its mission.

For this reason, the initial discussion and final approval of the mission must start with the governing authority since it will have the fundamental responsibility for assuring that the museum or historical organization is effectively carrying out its mission.

As we begin this discussion on the development of the mission statement, we must remember that the governing authority has several nondelegatable responsibilities:

- It sets the strategic direction of the organization.
- It accepts fiduciary responsibility for the organization's operational and capital costs, its collections, and its good name.
- It acts as a vehicle that connects the organization to the communities it serves.

A good mission statement strengthens all of these critical governance activities. It is impossible to set a strategic direction for the organization in the absence of a good mission statement; without a good mission statement, it will be difficult, if not impossible, to develop the kind of organization that will attract the funds necessary for its support, to know what kinds of collections materials are appropriate, and to avoid becoming an attic for old "stuff." And if there is not a unifying statement with the power to hold together all those responsible for the museum's performance, it will be impossible to connect to the communities the museum purports to serve. As the group legally responsible for the organization, the governing authority requires a clear mission statement to determine not only the focus of the organization's activities but their limits as well. Mission helps the organization identify those to whom it needs to listen, what it needs to listen to, and what it can reasonably do to respond. It is important to remember that any organization has boundaries, and going beyond those boundaries without thoughtful discussion puts the organization at risk.

That being said, the staff has an extremely important role to play in the development of a mission statement as well. It used to be said that the governing authority set the policies for an organization, and the staff carried them out. Today, we recognize that this would never work. The governing authority does not have the expertise or experience to set "policies" but does have the fundamental responsibility, with the senior staff, to set the organization's direction. And it is the staff that has the expertise and experience to put this strategic direction into all aspects of the day-to-day experience of running the organization. A successful organization is a partnership between staff and governing authority. Mission and vision provide direction to the partnership.

We have used several methods of developing mission statements, but the one that seems to have worked the best overall is that which brings everyone— board, staff, and occasionally important stakeholders together several times as the mission is being developed.

This serves several purposes, not the least of which is bringing together members of the board and staff for the most important discussions that will ever

TEXTBOX 3.2

The great management thinker, Peter Drucker, was a believer in continued focus on the fundamentals. He suggested that any organization could benefit from answering the following simple questions:

1. What business are you in?
2. Who is your customer?
3. How do you measure success?
4. What is the plan?

We think this advice remains very wise and very appropriate for museums and historical organizations.

take place in the organization. No matter the size of the organization, there is often a sense that the board somehow represents the elite and the staff are the minions, the doers, the clerks of the works, so to speak. We believe that it is critical for these two groups to speak of important things together. They have much to learn from each other, and bringing them together for important discussions invariably strengthens the organization.

Development of the mission statement is, as we said above, if somewhat differently, the most important thing the organization will ever do. For this reason, the process should not be rushed. Ample time must be provided for discussion by the governing authority; ample time must be provided for the governing authority to listen to the views of staff and key stakeholders and to engage them in conversation, whether individually or as a group. There will never be a better time to listen to and engage such an important cross section of thoughtful opinion about the organization and its fundamental purpose.

The development of an effective mission should be part of a more broadly conceived process of strategic planning. Strategic planning begins with mission. While other chapters in this volume deal in much more detail with the process of developing an organizational strategic plan, it is important to remember that, from a governance perspective, the development of the strategic plan is one of the most effective ways to stimulate, and in some cases force, a discussion of those things most important to the organization. And a discussion of mission should begin any strategic planning process.

It is important to understand that a good mission statement does not need to soar; it need not be lofty or catchy or describe the specific parts of the organization in any detail. One of the most frequent pitfalls for organizations in the development of their mission statement is that they feel the need to refer to specific collections, methods of interpretation, and other things that are in fact tools and strategies for carrying out the mission rather than the mission itself. First and foremost, the mission must be clear and concise. If it is, it can provide a strong platform upon which market positioning and branding statements, or taglines, can be built.

If you already have a mission, you must ask yourselves these questions: Do we have the right mission? Is it understood and fully supported by all members of the governing authority? Is it understood and fully supported by all members of the staff? Is it understood and fully supported by the key stakeholders? Without a discussion about mission, and ideally vision, it is impossible for an organization to arrive at appropriate strategic goals for the next, say, three to five years. And without a serious group discussion of mission and vision, unacknowledged issues, disagreements, and contrary viewpoints will continue to sleep comfortably beneath the surface, causing an array of symptoms and not a clue as to their cause.

So, mission comes first, vision comes second, and the strategic plan, with its goals and strategies, comes third.

We encourage our clients to think about mission in terms of the three key elements critical to the development of a good mission statement: (1) action, (2) outcome, and (3) value.

- *Action:* The organization has to do something that is distinctive and for which it has special skills and experience.
- *Outcome:* There must be a clearly articulated outcome for what the organization does.
- *Value:* Finally, a statement of the social value of the outcome of the action the organization provides is essential. It may be difficult to separate outcome from value since there is often a value implicit in the outcome of what the organization does. That is fine as long as its implicitness in the statement of outcome is clear.

Sometimes it is easier to see this concept through examples of invented mission statements from businesses unlike our own. In that way, we bring no baggage to the concept and open ourselves to the idea behind it. For example,

- *Mrs. Bee's Pie Palace makes fruit pies from low-fat organic ingredients, delightful to look at, delicious to taste, and we present them to our customers*

Our mission mantra is "action, outcome, and value."

as a no-guilt contribution to enjoyable and healthful living. In this case, Mrs. Bee's makes pies out of good ingredients (action); they taste and look good (outcome); they contribute to their customers' enjoyment and health (value).

- *The Wholesome Shoe Company designs and fabricates comfortable, stylish shoes that release the feet from strain and inspire the wearer to move through the day with renewed vigor and confidence.* The Wholesome Shoe Company makes good shoes (action) that release the feet from strain (outcome) and provide renewed vigor and confidence (value).

These are simplistic examples at best, but they do illustrate the point. Sometimes museums find it easier to talk about a commercial product than about what they do. But this should not be. We produce a product (our programs and exhibitions) for customers (our audiences), which must have value for them or why should they want it?

Our experience has been that governing authorities, and others to be sure, find talking about value the most difficult part of the mission discussion. Many will assert that the value of the organization is self-evident and needs no discussion. On closer examination, it becomes clear that individual board members have individual concepts of what the value of the organization is;

TEXTBOX 3.3

Here are several mission statements from historical museums that we think address action, outcome, and value:

- The Tenement Museum promotes tolerance and historical perspective through the presentation and interpretation of the variety of immigrant and migrant experiences on Manhattan's Lower East Side, a gateway to America.
- The Rosenbach Museum and Library seeks to inspire curiosity, inquiry, and creativity by engaging broad public audiences in exhibitions, programs, and research based on its remarkable and expanding collections.
- The Minnesota Historical Society connects people with history to help them gain perspective on their lives. The society preserves the past and tells the stories of Minnesota's people.

some may even see the organization as having several values, all of equal importance. What surfaces almost immediately, and what most participants see right away, is that there is no shared understanding about the organization, no shared sense of the importance of what it does, no shared sense of its value as an organization—a true anchor if ever there was one. And a light bulb switches on for most board members, who generally do not know there are so many differing views. Boards are, for the most part, quietly collegial, and important issues that may lead to personal conflict or disagreement are seldom discussed. We believe it is important to force that discussion. For how can we tell another person about the purpose and value of our organization if we do not know what it is ourselves, or if others who are equally important to the success of the organization hold different versions. Where is there solid ground on which to build and from which to plan? And how can we gain credibility with our audiences if they hear different versions of the "truth" from different members of the organization?

We have found that discussing mission in these terms forces the governing authority to talk about the basic and fundamental identity and value of the particular organization. For many organizations, it is the first time this type of discussion has taken place. Because the discussion of mission often brings the most deeply held convictions, and sometimes the most contentious issues, to the surface, it works best when facilitated and led by someone outside the organization. When the governing authority tries to facilitate the process internally, it is very difficult, if not impossible, for any individual member to bring up contentious issues of focus and direction. Having an outside individual who can ask uncomfortable questions and press the discussion of potentially contentious issues can be invaluable to the mission-creating process.

We have found that having something to look at and react to energizes participants in mission discussions to return to the table with renewed energy, and so, following in-depth discussions on the subject with members of the governing authority and staff, we often draft several versions of possible mission statements for them to consider. The same people who might never have been able to write a mission statement on their own will immediately recognize what is spot-on and what does not work for their organization, and they will begin a much more focused discussion that quickly results in an organizational mission all can embrace enthusiastically.

As museums and historical organizations reach out and engage, or try to engage, nontraditional audiences, it is essential that they be able to articulate, first and foremost to themselves, the value they claim to provide in order to be sure it is embodied in everything they do. If it is not, you can be sure your audiences will tell you, either directly or simply by not coming.

AN EXAMPLE OF A VISION STATEMENT

Each of the following statements represents a measureable snapshot of the museum at a future time if the mission is relentlessly pursued:

- The museum will have moved to a more appropriate facility and will have engaged in a successful fundraising campaign to support its capital costs.
- The museum will have sufficient contributed support and earned revenue to sustain its ongoing operating costs as well as desired program and infrastructure improvements.
- The museum will have an endowment fund of $5 million.
- The museum will be considered a "must-see" attraction for visitors to the area.
- The museum will be seen as an important center of community engagement with history and heritage by residents of the region.
- The museum will be known for delivering innovative, engaging, content-rich educational programs that are mission driven and audience focused.
- The museum will be known for its exemplary standards of welcome and hospitality.
- The museum collections will be considered a unique and important resource for documenting the history of the region from its beginnings up to the present day; the collections will be well housed and serve as a cultural reference point for researchers, residents, and visitors.
- The museum will be seen as an important educational resource by school districts throughout the region.
- The museum will have sufficient and appropriate staff to carry out its programs and activities effectively and efficiently.
- The museum staff will be acknowledged leaders and innovators in museum-based public interpretation and engagement.
- The museum will have a large and well-trained volunteer corps at a variety of age levels involved in every area of museum activity.
- The museum board will be strategically focused and fully committed to fulfilling its fiduciary and advocacy responsibilities in an ongoing way.
- The museum will be engaged in a variety of strategic partnerships and collaborations with other organizations to advance its mission.
- The museum will use Web-based technologies to provide information about its programs and access to its collections, as well as to create an online community of people interested in history.

We encourage you to look on the Web for the mission statements of other museums and historical organizations to see what many of your colleague organizations have developed. The successful outcome of the mission-statement-creation process will be a clear statement that is understood and agreed upon by all members of the governing authority. One more illustration of an invented mission follows:

> The museum creates a well-thought-out mission statement through a facilitated process (action) that is clear, understood, and agreed upon by all members of the governing authority (outcome) in order to assure programmatic and collecting focus and inspirational value to all its visitors (value).

Once the mission statement has been approved, the members of the governing authority must embrace it, or they should resign. Loyalty to the mission is one of the most fundamental responsibilities of any member of the governing authority. It is often the case that issues are raised and differences exposed through a series of discussions leading up to the development of an organization's mission statement. It may be that several members resign from the governing authority. If that is the case, the governing authority should allow those members to leave without protest. The organization will probably be stronger for it in the long run.

Our rule of thumb is that a mission statement needs to be short enough to fit on the back of a business card. If it is to be the organizational gyroscope, it needs to be in strong and visible evidence, and every member of the board and staff should be able to recite the mission easily, with understanding and enthusiasm.

Developing a Vision Statement

Closely related to mission is organizational vision. We see the statement of vision as a snapshot of the organization at a future point, perhaps two to eight years hence. The individual bullet points in a statement of vision articulate organizational aspiration and commit the organization to achieving certain quantifiable ambitions within a finite period. The vision can only be achieved if the mission is pursued through a well-thought-out strategic plan.

The vision statement is not a restatement of lofty goals but a description of individual attributes that can be measured at a particular time in the future. Taken together, the various specific targets noted in the vision statement provide an aspirational picture of the organization if it follows its mission over a reasonable period. Some examples of measurable components of a vision statement might include the following:

- The museum will have sufficient contributed support and earned revenue to provide for its necessary operating costs as well as desired program and capital improvements.

- The museum will be a must-see attraction for visitors to XYZ city.
- The museum staff will be seen by their peers as innovators and leaders in the field.
- The museum will be accredited by the American Association of Museums.

Defining a statement of vision is much easier than developing a mission statement. Perhaps this is because the discussions that lead to development of the mission have warmed participants to the process, and they are confident, newly enabled through discussions of depth and intensity, and ready to identify the much more specific organizational aspirations against which future success can be measured. And many of these will undoubtedly have been articulated as part of the earlier mission discussions, making the vision process that much easier.

Managing the Mission and Vision by the Governing Authority

Once the mission statement has been approved, it should become the yardstick against which everything the organization does is measured. It drives basic organizational goals and strategies and needs to be embedded in the structure and process of meetings of the governing authority. It has been our experience that, all too often, the meetings of the governing authorities of museums and historical organizations focus on informational reports (which could just as easily be distributed and read ahead of time) rather than strategic discussion. The result is that data drives out discussion, and the most important question—how are we doing in implementing our mission—goes unaddressed. How much better it would be to keep the governing authority and senior staff focused on big-picture issues that can engage them on a much higher level than monitoring the day-to-day operations and activities of the organization.

In partnership with mission, vision serves to remind board, staff, and stakeholders where they are headed and what they intend to achieve within a certain number of years. The vision provides the specificity of delineated measures of success: If the mission and the goals and strategies of a strategic plan are faithfully and enthusiastically followed, the vision gives a snapshot of what the organization will look like in x years.

Every aspect of the work of the organization must be directed toward fulfillment of mission and achievement of vision, and much within the organization may have to change. At the very least, everything must be looked at. For example, the committee structure of the governing authority may mirror or replicate the museum's operating structure. While such a structure can be quite appropriate for an organization in which the governing authority must provide necessary expertise and skill on a volunteer basis, we find that it often becomes entrenched, that board members are unwilling to let go of this structure long after the need for it has passed. This makes for a difficult work environment for professional staff whose decisions may be questioned by people with great interest and commitment, to be sure, but with little formal training in the area in question. Additionally, it may lead the museum to select board members based on particular interests or presumed skill sets rather than because they will be well equipped to move the museum forward in the areas of overall strategy and fundraising. It is not the governing authority's job to monitor the staff's performance of functional responsibilities (except in the case of the director); rather, the governing authority should monitor overall organizational performance against mission. For this reason, more and more museums and historical organizations are significantly reducing the number of standing committees and developing instead more strategically focused committees and task forces to work on specific strategic issues—and be dissolved once those issues have been addressed.

In working with client organizations, we often ask members of the governing authority and staff to sketch a basic organizational chart for us. Almost without fail, both put the governing authority at the top of the chart. This is a mistake. Once approved by the organization's governing authority, the mission can rightfully take its place at the top of the organizational chart. The mission, in conjunction with the strategic plan, which puts implementation of the mission into a series of strategies, can now provide a strong framework for organizing all of the work of the governing authority—and in turn the work of staff and other key stakeholders in the organization.

Mission answers the big question: "What is the purpose of the organization?" Vision answers the question, "What will the organization look like if we achieve our ambition?" This may seem simplistic, but in our work, we have come into contact with many organizations—big, small, and in between—where the governing authority and senior staff still spend a great deal of time spinning their wheels discussing what the organization should be doing. With an agreed-upon mission, the fundamentals are not in doubt and do not need to be discussed; discussions between the governing authority and senior staff can focus on means, not ends.

We suggest that, once developed, the mission statement be prominently displayed in the room where the governing authority meets so that it is a constant presence and reminder of why they are there.

The strategic plan, developed to implement the mission, should now form the agenda for formal meetings of the governing authority; the important work now is to assure that the organization is making progress on its plan and toward success in those aspirations it has set forth for itself in the vision. By this simple act, the meetings of the governing authority can be made much more strategically focused and efficient. Many organizations have found that individual board

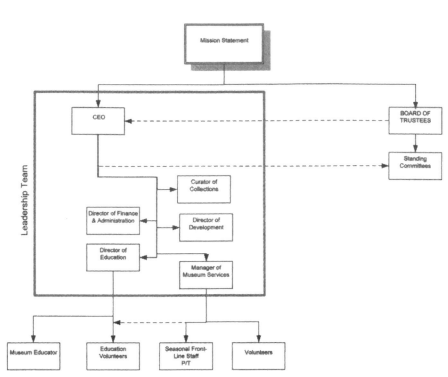

Organizational Chart

Mission Statement

CEO

BOARD OF TRUSTEES

Standing Committees

Leadership Team

Curator of Collections

Director of Finance & Administration

Director of Development

Director of Education

Manager of Museum Services

Museum Educator

Education Volunteers

Seasonal Front-Line Staff P/T

Volunteers

Figure 3.1. A sample of a basic organizational chart.

members who may have been bored and restless are energized by the specificity and focus of a strategic plan.

Once approved, the organizational mission and accompanying vision and strategic plan can be powerful recruitment tools for the governing authority. Busy and influential people want to be part of an organization whose mission they respect—and hopefully have a passion for. They want to be involved with an organization that will use their time effectively and efficiently. A strong mission, vision, and strategic plan can provide that assurance. And in an organization where the governing authority has a history of making appointments for political or personal reasons, a strong, clear mission, vision, and strategic plan can provide a powerful defense against these efforts.

We hope we have convinced you that development of a clear mission, vision, and strategic plan for your museum or historical organization is one of the most important responsibilities of the organization, most especially of its governing authority. These three documents provide the essential foundation for success in everything the organization does.

DIY STRATEGIC PLANNING[1]

Cinnamon Catlin-Legutko

In the spirit of do-it-yourself (DIY) television shows, this chapter offers a DIY approach to strategic planning. Developed in 2003 at the General Lew Wallace Study & Museum, a small museum and historic site, in Crawfordsville, Indiana, this approach is especially appealing to small museums as it costs little to no money to implement and can be completed in-house by existing staff or volunteers. This approach is also a good match for small museums as it accommodates nuts-and-bolts goals and projects that may not be as pertinent to other museums.

At its core, this planning template is rooted in basic project management, where it is important to determine tasks, resources, and deadlines ahead of a project's start date to lower the risk of failure. A strategic plan is really a form of project management. With a vision for your organization, an allocation of time for planning, public speaking ability, and a modicum of computer literacy, you can easily create a strategic plan that is embraced both internally by staff and externally by donors, grant makers, civic leaders, visitors, educators, and other interested parties.

Why Are Strategic Plans Needed?

A strategic plan, simply put, is a map or chart that an organization agrees to follow for three or five years in order to reach its goals. Institutions need strategic plans to help direct efforts and resources in an efficient and strategic manner. Responding to community and audience needs requires a strategic plan.

The planning process is strategic because you are establishing the goals that make the organization dynamic within its community and allow it to keep in step with the community's needs. It is systematic because it is focused and evaluative in choosing priorities. Institutions make decisions about short- and long-term goals and secure consensus. And most importantly, strategic planning is about building commitment and engaging stakeholders. Once the plan is in place, and you have met with all the stakeholders you can, you now have both the authority to complete the work and a direction to take.

Strategic plans are different from long-range or operational plans. Plans are strategic when the goals are responding to the museum's environment, seeking a competitive edge, and looking for the keys to long-term sustainability. Long-range or operational plans do not redefine the organization and position it in the community. These plans are more concerned with laying out immediate and future goals and are less concerned with organizational change. At the end of a five-year strategic plan, you will want to take the time to evaluate its success and consider next steps. If it was a complete success, changing course may not be necessary, and you simply need to plan the next five years along the same course. This would warrant a long-range or operational plan.

Through strategic planning, pen is put to paper, and major goals are defined. These goals may spur a sea change or a small shift in operations. It is important to realize at the beginning of the process that the strategic plan is the means to an end. It is a living document, and as such, opportunities that are good for the organization should be considered with the plan in mind but not completely disregarded because they are not "in the plan." The means are flexible, while the end is not.

Is Your Museum Ready for Strategic Planning?

Conditions must be right for strategic planning to begin. None of us has the time to waste on planning if the board does not support it or the goals are unachievable. In these circumstances, staff and board will ignore any attempt at a plan.

The proper strategic planning conditions depend on the organization, but the primary indicators for readiness include board and staff commitment and a vision for the future. There are two parts to guaranteeing the success of a strategic plan:

1. Creating a realistic strategy that matches current and anticipated resources.

> The strategic plan is the means (flexible) to an end (not flexible). It is a living document.

2. Ensuring that board and staff embrace the plan and agree on the articulated goals.

Before you get started, the director should evaluate organizational readiness. If the organization has serious issues—such as board infighting, major budgetary shortfalls, or cynicism regarding planning—take steps to resolve them before the process begins. Table 4.1 provides several statements to help you consider organizational readiness. Consider the statements provided in the left column of the table, and check whether your museum is ready or not. When selecting a no response, make a note about whom to consult with to consider resolution (e.g., the board president, executive committee, etc.). If you realize you are not ready based on two or more negative responses, use the considerations in the far-right column to determine how to get ready and when you might be able to begin strategic planning. If you cannot easily remedy these considerations, create an action plan based on your responses. Work with key individuals to execute that plan, and set a schedule for getting back to strategic planning.

If you are ready, consider whether you have any lingering comments or concerns that you want to capture and share with the appropriate committee or person before you proceed. It is essential to address these concerns up front. Otherwise, congratulations! You are now ready to begin the strategic planning process.

The Key Players

There are several individuals who should participate in the strategic planning process, but the actual number of participants and their function in the organization will vary from museum to museum. The goal should be to have all board members participate in the process, and depending on staff size, all or most of the staff should participate. It is also important to look beyond the internal players and think externally. The museum exists to serve the public, so what does the public want from your institution?

Depending on your museum's size, you could have the board, staff, and community leaders all sitting at the same table during the strategic planning process. But realistically, splitting these groups up might be better. You could hold a joint board and staff session and then hold one or more separate public focus groups, or you could hold three separate sessions. It primarily depends on what the plan facilitator or the museum director finds to be the best scenario for the organization.

Table 4.1. Is Your Organization Ready for Strategic Planning?

Readiness Issues	Yes. You are ready!	No. You need to fix/ review a few things first.	Considerations if not ready
The museum has enough money to pay bills over the next six months.			How can your museum get enough money? By when? Start strategic planning when?
The museum has a history of being able to plan and implement its plans.			What can be done to address this issue? Leadership development? Other ideas? Start strategic planning when?
Board members work well together. Staff members get along.			Problem in board? Problem with staff? What can be done? Start strategic planning when?
Board members are willing to be involved in top-level planning.			What can be done? Start strategic planning when?
Board members and staff will find the time to do the planning.			What can be done to free up more time? Start strategic planning when?
No major changes are expected in the next one to two months.			What changes? What can be done to get ready for strategic planning? By when?
There is extensive support for planning in your museum (internally and externally).			What can you do to address any cynicism? Start strategic planning when?
Strategic planning efforts are under way because the museum is ready for change and not just because a grantmaker or funder is asking for it.			What should you do about this? Start strategic planning when?

*Adapted from *Field Guide to Nonprofit Strategic Planning and Fundraising*, published by Authenticity Consulting, LLC.

TEXTBOX 4.1

STRATEGIC PLANNING IN ACTION

The Historical Society of Frederick County (Maryland) is no stranger to planning. Operating with five full-time employees and one part-time staff member, the society was founded in 1892 and is accredited by the American Association of Museums. With thorough assessment (Museum Assessment and Conservation Assessment Programs) and planning, the organization has grown tremendously since the hiring of its first director in the 1990s, resulting in a current annual budget of approximately $300,000.

At the time of this writing, the executive director, Heidi Campbell-Shoaf, shared that the society was in the middle of developing its next plan. For many years, the organization drafted long-range plans, and in 2006, it adopted its first strategic plan, which sunset in 2010. But the board and staff recognized that certain critical goals had not been fulfilled by the end of year five. They understood that a plan can only be effective if it is flexible, so the board adopted an interim plan to cover 2011 and 2012. This interim plan includes the remaining unfinished items and allows ample time for the next plan to develop. The board is to be applauded for realizing that the small museum environment and outside economic forces can conspire against a plan's timeline—creating this interim plan makes room for organizational success.

The interim plan was created by the members of the board of directors and staff during their annual planning retreat. After a review of the 2007–2010 plan, accomplished items were removed. Unmet or partially met goals remain in the update to guide activities for the next two years. While this was a simple updating process, the process for the 2007–2010 plan was more complex and involved several focus groups of different stakeholders in the community (e.g., business and government, education, and historical organizations) and surveys of historical society membership and staff. A facilitator was employed during the planning session, and the process was overseen by a committee of staff and board members. The intent is to replicate this process for the next five-year plan.

One goal of the 2007–2010 plan was to make the headquarters building (home to the museum and research center) more accessible to people with disabilities. Located in a historic structure with historic preservation easements on it, the society found making the building more accessible a challenge. With careful planning, it was able to install wheelchair access and

(continued)

TEXTBOX 4.1 (*Continued*)

a lift. Another accessibility solution was the creation of an online catalog of the research center and archival holdings. The society also established an endowment specifically for collections acquisitions relevant to its collections plan. These goals and many more were realized because of a well-constructed strategic plan.[1]

To learn more about the Historical Society of Frederick County, visit www.hsfcinfo.org.

Note

1. Heidi Campbell-Shoaf, e-mail message to author (adapted), March 24, 2011.

Creating the Plan

The following is a step-by-step outline for DIY strategic planning developed at the General Lew Wallace Study & Museum. Since its inception, this approach has been successfully implemented in other small organizations and produced the same results. While it was a complete success for us, you may want to adapt some of the steps to match your organizational behavior. For example, when we were getting started, the board members involved were unable to meet for a long period for a variety of reasons. To ensure that the process would get off the ground, we compromised and shortened the first session to three hours (instead of the six we really needed). By the next strategic planning cycle, the board was more accustomed to strategic thinking and implementing plans and spent more time around the table developing the next plan. (In fact, the board members gave up two Saturdays to work with a facilitator for the 2009–2013 plan.)

DIY strategic planning has three key processes: preparation, facilitation, and formatting.

Preparation

1. *Gain board support for strategic planning.* One of the key functions of the board is to set the strategic direction of the museum and ensure that the resources are in place to realize the goals. During the course of a regular board meeting, the board president should lead a discussion about strategic planning, the methods to be used, what is expected of board members, and how much time the process will take. Once the groundwork is in place, the president should call for a motion to proceed with strategic planning. During that meeting, you should set the date for the first session.

2. *Select a project leader or facilitator.* The museum director serves as the project leader or facilitator in the absence of funding for a consultant. While it is better to have an independent party facilitate brainstorming activities and guide the overall process (this allows the director to participate more fully and prevents the director from being heavy-handed), this is sometimes not feasible in a small museum. To make sure that he or she has input into the process, the director may meet with board members before the meeting, share ideas, and encourage them to keep these ideas coming during later brainstorming opportunities.

3. *Determine the length of the plan.* Decide along with the board whether this will be a three- or five-year plan. There is no magic formula for deciding the plan's length. In the case of the General Lew Wallace Study & Museum, we chose five years because the board and director knew that resources would support a five-year plan, and we knew that the amount of change needed to improve operations would be better effected by a five-year plan. However, we left the fifth year open and assigned no formal tasks, specifically for the purpose of leaving room for scope and time line changes. During the strategic planning process, the staff consisted of only two part-time, seasonal employees, the director included. As the implementation of the plan gained momentum, the board and staff worked together to negotiate deadlines and adjust the scope to fit resources. By year three of the plan, the fifth year was full of tasks.

If you are an all-volunteer organization, a three-year plan might be more suitable. Volunteer energy needs to be replenished more frequently, and the planning process can be a tool for reenergizing and refocusing. An organization with board members who are not completely convinced about strategic planning may choose three years to demonstrate organizational potential. Experts do not recommend plans shorter than three years because it takes at least three years for many changes to take root and for resources to align with strategic areas.

4. *Identify five organizational categories.* Identifying categories from the outset will help frame the overall planning process and the later brainstorming activity. You will need to distill museum functions and projects into five categories at most: education, administration, collections, and so forth. These categories can be broad umbrella terms or "hot-topic" issues pertinent to your organization, such as interpretation, a community initiative, or a major event (e.g., a centennial commemoration). To guarantee the development of a feasible plan, limit it to five categories and use them as guideposts during the planning process and as the backbone of the final plan.

At the General Lew Wallace Study & Museum, we used the categories of administration, education, collections management, building/grounds preservation, and development. For our purposes, exhibits, educational programming, and guided tours are all under the education umbrella because their ultimate intent is to educate the public. Development includes fundraising, public rela-

WARM-UP WORKSHEET

Develop a worksheet that asks these questions:

1. What is your vision for the museum?
2. List five things you would like to see happen at the museum that will help make this vision a reality.
3. Where do you see yourself in this vision?
4. Where do you see the museum in five years?

tions, marketing, and staff training because these efforts develop the overall sustainability and visibility of the site. For the General Lew Wallace Study & Museum, these categories were most relevant in 2003, but in 2008, when we developed the next plan, the categories changed.

5. *Distribute a warm-up activity.* Before the first scheduled strategic planning session, distribute a worksheet to the participants to help them start thinking about the future of the organization and prepare them for the brainstorming session. You can e-mail or mail the worksheet and instruct them to complete it and bring it with them to the first session.

Facilitation

1. *Convene a brainstorming session.* Ideally, the first gathering should be a five-hour session with a clear agenda provided ahead of time. During this first gathering, the lion's share of board work is completed. Board members will share ideas, think of new ones, and begin placing them into concise statements.

For this first session, you will need two flip charts (preferably the kind with adhesive) and several colors of markers. Do not use a chalkboard or dry-erase board. You need to keep the notes throughout the entire planning process—you will refer to them during the second strategic planning session, and you will need them as you draft the plan. Plus, it is always a good idea to keep the evidence.

2. *Begin with an icebreaker exercise.* Although it may sound and feel corny, an icebreaker exercise is always a good way to make everyone comfortable and ready to begin. If you choose the right icebreaker, you can learn something about the participants. Go around the room, and ask them what the last museum they visited was (it cannot be yours) and why. You will learn something about what drives participants to go to a museum, what kinds of museums they like, and

TEXTBOX 4.3

SAMPLE GROUND RULES

1. There are *no* bad ideas!
2. One person speaks at a time.
3. Listen when another participant speaks. Give him or her the floor.
4. Think about small, medium, and large ideas. No idea is too small.
5. Allow yourself to be inspired by another participant's idea.
6. When thinking of ideas, visualize yourself as a board member, a staff member, a volunteer, a museum visitor, and a donor.

how far they will travel to visit a museum. Or you will find out that some of them have no relationship to museums other than the one they serve. Both types of responses can be very enlightening.

3. *Present the ground rules.* Adults need ground rules as much as children do. To keep the group charged with positive energy and encouragement, cover the ground rules and post them on a wall in the meeting room. Refer to the rules throughout the process to help control behavior issues. At no point do you want anyone to feel alienated, threatened, or discouraged. The brainstorming process works best when everyone is firing off ideas and working in a respectful manner.

4. *Work in pairs.* Before you start the open brainstorming segment, divide the group into pairs. Be sure to pair up people who may not know each other very well or who rarely have the opportunity to work together. Send them to various locations (outside, down the hall, in the corner) with the "Before-the-Storm Worksheet" (see textbox 4.4). This worksheet is designed to build confidence among participants, drill down the ideas, and begin the visioning process. At the end of the exercise, the pair will condense their ideas into five strategic goals.

5. *Brainstorm as a group.* The purpose of the group brainstorm is to gather as many ideas as possible, capture them on paper, and keep everyone engaged and excited about them. Very simply, facilitation is about helping a group of people reach their goals. During the course of the brainstorming session, the facilitator will

- control the meeting;
- set and enforce rules;
- ensure participation;
- allow for flow of thought;
- keep the ball rolling;
- keep the meeting on topic;

TEXTBOX 4.4

SAMPLE "BEFORE-THE-STORM WORKSHEET"

For the purposes of this strategic plan, we are using five predetermined categories of museum management and operation: administration, collections management, education, building/grounds preservation, and development.

1. Working with a partner, consider these categories and create a vision for the museum. What kind of museum will it be in five, ten, fifteen years? When the vision is realized, what will the museum be like for the visitor? This should be one sentence that imagines "a day in the life of the visitor" and makes a promise.
2. Use the vision and quickly brainstorm ideas that can make the vision a reality. These will be your notes for the group brainstorming session, which will ultimately reveal the main components of the strategic plan.
3. Finally, turn the sheet over and drill your brainstorm ideas down into five main strategic goals. You can come up with more if necessary.

You will have thirty minutes to complete this activity.

- act generally as a nonparticipant;
- be a subject matter expert;
- accurately sum up discussion;
- smile as much as humanly possible.

Brainstorming sessions are fast, exciting, and creative. To warm the group to the challenge, you may start the session with a mock brainstorm. Ask participants to share ideas about what constitute the great moments in American history or the best movies of all time. Not only will newcomers to the process get the opportunity to see how it works (and you will get a chance to practice), but you will also see who the talkers and the wallflowers are. This also helps you keep the conversation balanced and watch for domineering personality types.

Once the ball is rolling, these steps will take you through the process and help you gather the most salient points:

- Jot ideas onto flip charts while keeping ideas flowing.
- Once momentum has slowed, review ideas for clarity and ask for a show of hands of how many people had identified these ideas on

worksheets ahead of time. (You can mark the number of hands next to each item to show consensus; items with the most hash marks should receive the highest priority in the plan.) This quick break will likely inspire more brainstorming. Be sure to keep it going while participants are hot.

- During a food break, categorize the brainstorm list on separate flip chart sheets. Before getting started, write each operational category on a separate flip chart sheet (e.g., collection management). As an alternative, you can run through the lists and code the ideas into categories (i.e., *D* for development, *E* for education, etc.).

- Once everyone has eaten and had a break, reconvene the group to consider the categories and how you assigned them. Look for gaps. Did participants come up with a million programming ideas but never mention collections care? You can take time at this point to restart the brainstorm if there are some obvious holes.

1. *Initial visioning session:* Once the brainstorming period has slowed down, it is time to start developing a vision statement. A vision statement focuses on the future and considers what the museum will look like down the road (what the visitor experience will be like, how the museum will function). The vision statement incorporates the needs and desires of the board and staff and crystallizes them into a picture of the future. For some, it is simply a version of the question, "What do you want to be when you grow up?" This first visioning session will start with a conversation, resulting in a first draft of a vision statement. To start the discussion, it is useful to create a word list on flip charts about what the board values and what the museum can offer. Having a pool of words to refer to is helpful when drafting a statement.

TEXTBOX 4.5

SHOPPING LIST

Snacks and beverages
Lunch or dinner
Flip charts (at least two)
Easels (two)
Open wall space

Markers, two to three colors
Masking tape
Ink pens
Tent cards (for participant names)

2. *Follow-up session:* Before the participants leave the first session, establish the date and time of the follow-up session. Try to get a sense of how many people will attend the second session, which will last about two hours. (For some reason, no matter what you do, you should expect fewer participants for this second session.)

During the follow-up session, the facilitator presents the first draft of the plan and walks the group through the initial format. This draft will include ideas from the first brainstorming session and formalized strategic goals. It may also include proposed time lines and anticipated resources. This is another opportunity for idea clarification and consideration of the priorities and time line.

Once the group approves the first report, return to the vision statement drafted in the first session. Does it still hold water? Does anyone have any revisions? If they do, take the appropriate amount of time to work with the wording, but do not allow the conversation to drag out longer than thirty minutes. You will want spend the bulk of your time in the session on developing the mission statement.

The mission statement is the most important series of words the board will consider, develop, and approve. It defines the purpose of the organization, answering why you are here and why the museum matters to its visitors and community. The board must believe in and enforce the mission. While the vision looks to the future, the mission establishes why the museum should continue, and the strategic plan determines how it will reach the future. Your current mission statement might be aligned with your plan's direction, but the board needs to review and consider it during this process. If you decide to write a new one, it may be helpful to refer to the same list of words that the group used to develop the vision statement. Another excellent source of inspiration is to evaluate what visitors and program participants regularly say about the museum. What inspiration do they feel? What questions do they frequently ask?

Just like in the first session, you will want the participants to leave the table with a draft mission statement in their notes. At the next regularly scheduled board meeting, present the final draft of the plan for approval and ask the board to formally adopt the new mission statement.

Overall, the strategic planning process can take between four and twelve months. At the General Lew Wallace Study & Museum, we began planning in May and approved the final plan in September. For us, this short time frame was essential because we had a great deal of nuts-and-bolts work to do immediately, and the director wanted as much authority as possible to accomplish the work. The strategic plan allowed that to happen.

Formatting

The final document is simply a formal plan that speaks about the organization's value and makes a case for its future. The document outlines the organizational goals and spells out what steps will be taken to realize them. Once formalized, this document should be shared with community stakeholders, donors, political leaders, volunteers, and whoever is interested in the plan. Post it on your website. Create an abbreviated version of it, and turn it into a brochure. Make presentations in your community sharing the exciting news that your plan has produced.

The format of your plan will be as follows:

- *Introduction:* Provide information regarding how the plan was developed, who participated, and what the time frame was.
- *History of the organization:* Start from the beginning. How did your museum develop? What are some of the milestones in its development? The strategic plan is used as a way to build awareness of your organization and attract support for what you do. The whole picture needs to be presented.
- *Vision and mission statements:* This section simply lists the vision and mission statements on a single page.
- *Strategic goals:* After the first brainstorming session, the director will synthesize the ideas and themes into broadly stated strategic goals. All of the activities and projects that the group decides to implement will have a relationship with these larger strategic goals. This section requires the director to have some personal vision for the organization.
- *Evaluation:* A plan works best when the board and staff refer to it and regularly evaluate its progress. Explain how you will track and measure the impact (see "Tracking and Measuring the Plan" in the next section).
- *Implementation schedule:* The staff develops, and the board approves as part of the entire plan, the last three sections. You may want to involve key board members in the process of assigning tasks, solutions, responsibilities, and deadlines, if desired. In this section, indicate the priority of the project. You will likely have some projects that are urgent or have the resources needed to accomplish them. Assign these projects the highest priority. Other excellent ideas might currently have unclear funding sources and postponing them will not affect operations or endanger anyone or anything. This type of project will have a lower priority rating. The key here is to pick realistic time frames—estimate on the high side—and, whenever possible, to assign responsibility to a person, not a committee.

- *Task lists:* To understand better what the institution will accomplish year to year, you can reorganize the implementation schedule into a listing of projects and activities by year and quarter. In this format, the board and staff can track progress more clearly.
- *Action plans:* Used for major project and budget planning, action plans drill down details even further and are helpful tools for the board to review. A good action plan identifies the strategic goal being addressed, solutions, action steps, deadlines, responsible parties, costs, and outcome measurements. In the final draft of the strategic plan, only include a template of an action plan. Create a new action plan each time you launch a project.

When the Plan Is Ready

Tracking and Measuring the Plan

Once the plan is in place and formally approved, track and measure its progress on a regular basis. Keeping tabs on the plan is a major concern of the board and staff, and a formal reporting mechanism is useful. At the General Lew Wallace Study & Museum, we used the task list and inserted status updates on an annual or biennial basis. The board formally approves the revised task list each time.

On a bimonthly basis, the director's report to the board is formatted to include each strategic goal, and every item reported is placed underneath one of the goals. The staff also reviews the plan two to three times per year and makes adjustments to the regular work plan if needed. At year-end, tasks not completed are modified with a new deadline and justification for the change. This flexibility is essential because of the small staff size and funding limitations.

From the start of the plan in September 2003 to April 2006, we met 68 percent of our goals. With the completion of a major capital project in 2006, we reached 81 percent of our goals with over a year left in the five-year plan.

General Lew Wallace Study & Museum Strategic Plan Achievements

- We adopted a new name and developed an identity for the museum.
- The board of trustees restructured and grew from five members to thirteen.
- Fundraising efforts resulted in a 187 percent increase in income for the first twelve months. The consecutive year netted similar results.
- Staff size increased from two part-time, seasonal employees to two full-time and two part-time employees.

- We completed the Carriage House Interpretive Center, a full-service office and exhibit complex located in General Wallace's 1875 carriage house. This major capital project utilized nearly $250,000 in donations and grants.
- The museum introduced and sustained new and innovative annual programs, including the Lew Wallace Youth Academy, the Artists-in-Residence Program, and the Winter Historic Preservation Workshop Series.
- Each year, we offer special programming inspired by the annual exhibit theme for a variety of audiences.
- Museum visitation has increased by 10 percent or more each year since 2003.

Beyond the First Plan

DIY strategic planning is best used as the first strategic plan for a small museum. If you have implemented the first plan's goals and strengthened your organizational capacity, the board and staff have greater options available when developing the second plan. For example, you may choose to use an outside consultant to facilitate and draft a new strategic plan. Unbiased facilitation is always recommended, and you may decide to hire an outside facilitator the second time around. Most importantly, with a fully implemented initial plan, chances are you can afford to pay for help when it is time for the second plan!

Variations in the Process

This approach is tailored to the smallest of museum staffs and boards. At the General Lew Wallace Study & Museum, we were a mighty bunch of two staff members and five board members using the approach. This model will work for larger board and staff sizes, but if the group becomes larger than eighteen to twenty people, I suggested you break up the group. You could brainstorm and create vision and mission statements with the board (with a few staff members participating) and then separately with the staff. Follow this with a session with the board where you bring the perspectives of both camps together and look for differences and similarities. This approach is especially helpful when looking for disconnects in the organization.

Another variation is the use of community focus groups to gauge community interest in and perspectives about the organization. With a smaller staff and board, include community members in the entire planning process and have everyone work through it together. Or, if too many individuals are involved, hold independent strategic planning sessions and limit them to brainstorming.

STRATEGIC PLANNING IN ACTION

Operating with a staff of seven part-time employees and a budget just under $250,000, the Los Alamos Historical Society in Los Alamos, New Mexico, has just completed its first strategic plan. Developed in 2005, the process was inspired by a strategic plan from a nearby art center. The planning process included a strengths, weaknesses, opportunities, and threats (SWOT) analysis that resulted in eight strategic areas. Attended by board and staff, the plan was developed internally, and frustratingly, some parts of it were never completed. For example, the group members knew they wanted to increase shop sales and museum visitation, but target numbers were never plugged into the plan. Another deficiency of the old plan is that it tended to be more tactical than strategic.

Nevertheless, the society's assistant director, Heather McClenahan, shared that the plan was a roadmap for success, and it is gratifying to look back and see that they accomplished a great deal. One of the major accomplishments has been in the area of historic preservation. A 1913 log cabin that was moved to the historic district in 1985 has now been completely restored and, for the first time, interpreted. Another major accomplishment was the turnaround of the museum shop, which was bleeding cash in 2006. By 2008, the shop was temporarily closed and remodeled. A new manager was hired, and the shop went from a money loser to a moneymaker for the society. Lastly, significant increases in the society's advertising and marketing budgets have resulted in higher visitation numbers and increased sales in the shop.

The new plan, which is still in the planning phase, kicked off as the 2005 plan was reaching the end of its useful life. Notably, the society had recently participated in the Museum Assessment Program of the American Association of Museums, and the assessor recommended the development of a new strategic plan.

Beginning in the spring of 2010, the board of directors appointed a steering committee to oversee the drafting of a new plan. The committee includes three board members and one staff member. Simultaneously, the society was planning for a symposium on making the Oppenheimer House, one of the society's properties, a public history institution. The consultant for this symposium additionally agreed to facilitate the annual retreat, which generated ideas for the new strategic plan. The daylong retreat with board, staff, and key community members was held off-site in a historically inspired setting. After the retreat, staff compiled the retreat notes, and the steering committee refined the mission statement and narrowed down seven strategic directions. However, the vision statement was a struggle. The consultant wrote up some suggestions, but the three pages, while exciting, did not meet the board's desire for a simple statement. After much brain storming, e-mailing back and forth, and meeting, the steering committee hit upon a vision, which was the society's first.

Currently, subcommittees (chaired by board and staff members and including people from outside the board) are working on each of the seven strategic goals. Their work should be complete by the end of March 2011. The board will finalize the draft plan at its April 2011 meeting and present it to the membership at the annual meeting on May 2011. Because of the length of time it will cover (nearly six years), the intent is for the plan to be a living document, able to be adjusted as a new archives facility is built, the Oppenheimer House is opened to the public, and so much more. In the end, the planning process will have taken one year to complete.[1]

To learn more about the Los Alamos Historical Society, visit www.losalamoshistory.org.

Notes
1. Heather McClenahan, e-mail message to author (adapted), March 3, 2011

During the last thirty minutes of the session, field-test the new vision and mission statements to see if they resonate with the public.

Managing Change

If this is the first strategic plan for your organization, you are facing a great deal of change over the next few years. Being sensitive to stakeholders and processes is half the battle when managing change. Once you decide to make a change, it is important to think through its impact and do some troubleshooting. With a little thoughtful examination at the outset, the important changes you are making will last.

To orchestrate major changes at the General Lew Wallace Study & Museum, we used charters and change documents borrowed from standard project management methodology. Both of these tools open up communication channels and document the change. When appropriate, the board will formally approve the document, thereby endorsing the change. Everyone starts out—literally and figuratively—on the same page.

- *Charters:* Charters are documents that outline responsibilities and structures, and they are tools for managing people, projects, and change. At the General Lew Wallace Study & Museum, we use them primarily to define the purpose and goals of the board and ad hoc committees. With a charter, we make committee members aware of why they are there, chart out planned changes, promote accountability, and define budgetary impact. A charter typically outlines and defines eleven components: project/committee overview, scope, objectives, relevant strategic goals, measures/deliverables, budget, customers, boundaries, milestones, deadlines, and supporting documentation.

- *Change documents:* These reports can be used to makes a case for change to the board, stakeholders, and government entities. The format we used at the General Lew Wallace Study & Museum defined the statement of need, the current state, and the future state. It also offered a proposal, time line, cost-benefit analysis, barriers, and final recommendation.

Both documents demonstrate that you have done your homework and considered the impact of proposed changes on the organization. Essentially, if you cannot define what is requested in a charter or change document, you need to reconsider making the change.

Conclusion

This chapter offers one approach to strategic planning. Other museum and nonprofit professionals may stress varying approaches, including strengths, weaknesses, opportunities, and threats (SWOT) analysis, more extensive visioning sessions, longer time frames, and the like. As a small museum director, I found that I really did not need to be that reflective the first time. And with just two staff members working part-time, we were always on the front line testing what visitors wanted and making quick decisions to meet needs. In addition, in the fast-paced small museum environment, we needed this first plan in place as fast as possible so we could make major board-mandated changes to improve operations.

In developing a strategic plan, it is really time for "first things first." What will it take to do *x*? What will it take to do *y*? Where do we start? Invariably, it always ends up with fundraising and development. If you do not have income, much less a sustainable income source, how can you do innovative programming and exhibits or improve collections care? If you are struggling with time frames and prioritizing tasks, maybe it would be lbest to prioritize the development goals first. With the completion of a strategic plan, you have a strong case for support. Use it.

TEXTBOX 4.7

ABOUT THE GENERAL LEW WALLACE STUDY & MUSEUM, CRAWFORDSVILLE, INDIANA

The General Lew Wallace Study & Museum is a National Historic Landmark site owned and operated by the city of Crawfordsville and governed by the Lew Wallace Study Preservation Society, a 501(c)(3). The centerpiece of the site is the eclectic freestanding study designed by Gen. Lew Wallace (1827–1905). Best known as the author of *Ben-Hur*, Wallace was a Renaissance man and notable Hoosier. Inside the study and the newly rehabilitated Carriage House Interpretive Center, the museum houses personal mementos from his service as a Civil War major general, second officer of the Lincoln conspiracy military tribunal, governor of the New Mexico Territory (1878–1881), and U.S. minister to Turkey (1881–1885). Wallace's artwork, violins, inventions, and library are on display, along with memorabilia from various adaptations of *Ben-Hur*, including the 1959 Oscar-winning version starring Charlton Heston. The museum is located in downtown Crawfordsville on 3.5 acres of wooded grounds enclosed by a brick wall.

Upon Wallace's death in 1905, the Wallace family opened the study as a museum and operated it until 1939. The city of Crawfordsville has owned the property since 1941. Today, annual visitation is over seven thousand, with an annual budget of around $145,000. A full-time director and associate director, two part-time employees, and a small corps of volunteers staff the museum. Programs are offered year-round, including the popular Lew Wallace Youth Academy, the fall Artists-in-Residence Program, and a variety of themed programming in support of temporary exhibits. The museum also hosts the annual Taste of Montgomery County, a fundraiser for the Preservation Society.

In 2008, the museum was awarded the National Medal for Museum Service by the Institute for Museum and Library Services, making it one of the smallest museums ever to win, and the second museum in Indiana to receive, this distinguished honor.

Special Thanks

I am especially grateful to Heidi Campbell-Shoaf and Heather McClenahan for sharing their institutional examples and to Larry Paarlberg, director of the General Lew Wallace Study & Museum since 2009, for his review of this chapter.

Recommended Resources

Alliance for Nonprofit Management: www.allianceonline.org.

Brainstorming. "How to Do Traditional Brainstorming." Brainstorming. www.brain storming.co.uk/tutorials/howtobrainstorm.html.

Bryson, John M., and Farnum K. Alston. *Creating and Implementing Your Strategic Plan: A Workbook for Public and Nonprofit Organizations.* 2nd ed. San Francisco: Jossey-Bass, 2005.

Lord, Gail Dexter, and Kate Markert. *The Manual of Strategic Planning for Museums.* Lanham, MD: AltaMira Press, 2007.

McNamara, Carter. *Field Guide to Nonprofit Strategic Planning and Facilitation.* Minneapolis: Authenticity Consulting, LLC, 2003.

Merritt, Elizabeth E., and Victoria Garvin, eds. *Secrets of Institutional Planning.* Washington, DC: American Association of Museums, 2007.

Skramstad, Harold, and Susan Skramstad. *Handbook for Museum Trustees.* Washington, DC: American Association of Museums, 2003.

Strategic Planning for Smaller Nonprofit Organizations: www.wmich.edu/nonprofit/ Guide/guide7.htm.

Note

1. This revised manuscript was originally published as "DIY Strategic Planning for Small Museums," *History News* (Nashville) (spring 2008): 1–8.

"THOUSANDS OF SMALL GOOD ACTIONS": SUCCESSFUL MUSEUM GOVERNANCE
Teresa Goforth

If there is to be a strengthening of the nonprofit section . . . it must come about through thousands of small good actions by those who govern our many nonprofit organizations. Board members have special opportunities to bring about change, but to do so they must understand their core responsibilities and appreciate the importance of consistent and thoughtful interpretation of those responsibilities.[1]

Small museums are the most democratic of museum organizations; they can and should represent the many layers of a community and respond to its most important needs. Ideally, in a museum with or without paid staff, the board of directors is recruited to be representative of both the needs of the museum and the needs of its community, two things that hopefully are not mutually exclusive. Good museum governance requires the right chemistry of people and expertise, as well as a shared passion for the mission of the museum. This chapter provides a context for governance, outlines specific rules and responsibilities, and offers suggestions, tools, and resources to support a path to successful governance, which is a most important piece of a successful museum.

What Is Governance?

The *Oxford English Dictionary* gives as its first definition of the word governance "the action or manner of governing."[2] It sounds so straightforward and simple; yet it is very complex and critical to the success of an organization. Any museum, no matter how small, can create and sustain a successful governing structure, a key factor in developing or growing a successful museum, a cornerstone to community. Museum governance is a personal as well as a shared responsibility.

While there are many models of governance from which to choose, no single model will definitely fit all organizations. Often, a combination of various models works best for a given museum. When determining which model is best, the board must take into account a number of factors, including the following:

- size of staff, if any;
- resources and capabilities of board members and staff;
- board personality.

It is very common in the small museum world for a board to spend many years as a "working board"; then it may transition into some combination of a "working board" and a "policy board" if it has the good fortune to be able to grow and to hire staff in the future.

A working board is one whose members are also responsible for the day-to-day management of the museum (i.e., the care of collections, development of exhibitions, and presentation of educational programs). A policy board concerns itself only with the establishment of official policies for the organization, which the staff implements while taking responsibility for the day-to-day management of the organization. (A discussion of basic policies can be found later in this chapter on page 105.) The following case study of a small Michigan museum illustrates how a museum's governance model might change over time.

Case Study

This small museum, located in a rural community of about eight thousand people, in a prominent historic structure in the center of town, preserves and interprets the history of the county. It, like many small county historical museums, was founded in 1976 as a part of the county's bicentennial celebration. It began collecting and presenting exhibits and programs to the public. The historical society, in the early 1990s, became a nonprofit organization created to preserve the historic structure, develop the museum beyond its historical society roots, and fundraise to hire a professional staff person. The board did all the work of the museum for a couple of years, then successfully hired a young museum professional to take on that work, in partnership with the board of directors.

When the organization first began, the board was very clear in its responsibilities for the museum. Its foremost task was to raise funds to bring the building into better repair and to hire someone to manage the museum, preferably someone with museum experience. While doing this, it understood that it also needed to maintain efforts to care for the artifacts and open the doors at least once in awhile to the public. In organizing to take on a significant capital campaign in a small rural community, the board first had to look around at its members and determine the strengths and weaknesses of those at the table. It was clear that some had excellent connections in the community and no fear of asking for money; others were excellent organizers; some were extremely uncomfortable asking for dollars but were great writers, or had a passion for the building and its collections, or were not afraid to sell fundraising commodities such as memorial bricks. Each person on the board had a role to play, and that role was chosen based on his or her strengths, abilities, and resources. The museum board at this stage was a working board. In other words, the members of the board shared all the responsibilities for the management of the organization. Together, without the assistance of paid staff, this board raised nearly $250,000 in its small rural community.[3]

Once the board hired its executive director, a young professional who had recently completed her master's degree, the board had to reexamine its governing model and take into account how it would continue to work with staff, even a staff of just one. This can be a very difficult transition for both board and staff. Eventually, the board fell into a model that mixed a number of ideas, including roles for board members as policymakers responsible for oversight of the executive director; at the same time, the model also allowed them to continue to serve the organization in their working-board capacity as volunteers who functioned as partners with, and sometimes under the direction of, the executive director. In addition, though perhaps not explicitly stated, board members and staff developed a relationship as partners in the success of the museum. While this spirit faltered at times with certain personalities, most of the time the organization could grow and run smoothly because all of those involved worked on the premise that they were at the table for the same reason: the good of the museum.

Most small museums, by necessity, are governed by working boards because there is no one else there to do the work. This means that board members must fill multiple roles, swinging between establishing policies and taking care of the day-to-day work of the museum. It is very important that board members, when meeting and making decisions as a board, have a clear sense of identity. Some organizations, in order to have a clear sense of roles and responsibilities, actually create and approve a governance model or governance policy. The following is an example of one created for an organization with a single staff member.

> The Anytown Historical Museum Board of Directors governs and oversees operations through its bylaws, other board-approved policies, and a system of committees, which requires substantial involvement from the board members. The board delegates management functions to the executive director.

In drafting the statement above, the museum takes into consideration the following:

1. Our bylaws provide the only written source of direction (policy) to the organization. This document is regularly reviewed and updated to reflect any governance changes in the organization.
2. The Anytown Historical Museum has only one professional staff member, meaning that many of the goals of the museum are achieved

through its committees, which require active participation from board members in collaboration with the executive director.

3. The task of managing the decisions made by the committees is delegated to the executive director, who has considerable authority to achieve the stated goals. After a board or committee decision is made and the task is delegated to the executive director, any board member who assists with this task works under the direction of the executive director.[4]

Having a governance model or policy that has been approved by the board can be helpful because it limits any ambiguity there might be about the roles everyone plays in the organization and, ultimately, who is responsible for the oversight of the organization. The first and most important priority of the board of directors is to establish and oversee the implementation of those policies that keep the organization stable, responsible, and safe from liabilities as they relate to finances, the artifact collections, public safety, and education and programs.

Board Development and Maintenance

Many times, small museum boards are made up of folks who have been a part of the board for decades and sometimes feel as though they are the only ones who might want to be on the board. Small museums and historical societies sometimes behave as though they are awkward, perhaps brainy or nerdy, high school kids who feel like the popular kids certainly would not want to play with them. In reality, small community museums are the keepers of the heritage and memory of a community; that is an important thing to be. With that role comes responsibility and even a certain amount of power. Recruiting board members and keeping them for a reasonable length of time requires existing board members to think strategically and seek out those individuals who have skills and talents to bring to the organization. It also requires that they be excellent ambassadors for the organization, prepared to talk about board service as an honor and an opportunity, never using the phrase "We're really desperate for members," and ready to answer questions accurately and completely. This, like almost everything else boards do, requires prior thought and planning.

The first step in seeking out excellent board members is looking inward. If you have a strategic plan in place, look at your goals, objectives, and priorities to determine what qualities in a board member could help you meet those goals and objectives. For example, one of your organizational goals might be to increase the number of school groups that visit your museum. One effective way to do that is to build a strong relationship with people in your local school districts. While a teacher might be able to help build this relationship, a superintendant, curriculum director, or principal might have a broader reach and greater insight into how the museum could reach the broadest audience possible. Who on the existing board either knows someone in the school district or someone who knows someone? That person will become the liaison to the potential board member.

The identification of potential board members should be a group exercise. As a group you have outlined your needs, then identified and discussed specific people in the community who possess the necessary skills and, very importantly, the personalities that will allow them to be collaborative members of the organization. In most cases, the museum will have a nominating committee to refine this work. Members of the board can recommend potential board members to the nominating committee, which will be responsible for making contact with those individuals or identifying the most appropriate person to make contact. For small museums that have a paid executive, the staff person should not be left out of the nominating process. Often, because they are working with the public and organizational partners on a daily basis, they will come into contact with excellent prospective board members.

The director should not be excluded from the board-building process. In fact, there may be times when he or she is the best choice to make the initial contact with a possible future board member. The nominating committee has identified the appropriate board member, staff person, or museum friend to make contact with the individual who might make an excellent future board member. Create a small packet of information that explains who you are and why you matter to the community for the person making contact to take along. Explain why the prospective member cannot possibly pass up this opportunity to participate, and make sure you provide the information he or she needs to understand the commitment. A prospective board member packet should include the following items:

- A promotional piece about the museum
- A copy of the bylaws
- A copy of the most recent financial statement
- A summary of strategic goals if you have them
- A list of upcoming meeting dates or a description of when and how often the board meets
- A copy of a letter of commitment (see textbox 5.1)

By taking these initial steps up front, a museum lays the groundwork for a successful relationship with new board members. So much of what we do is

TEXTBOX 5.1

ANYTOWN HISTORICAL MUSEUM: BOARD MEMBER LETTER OF COMMITMENT[1]

As a board member of the Anytown Historical Museum (AHM), I understand my responsibilities are to

- be knowledgeable about the museum and committed to its mission and goals;
- serve as an advocate for the museum in the community and beyond;
- identify prospective board members and cultivate them when appropriate;
- participate in, volunteer for, and attend appropriate museum programs and events;
- actively serve on at least one standing board committee or serve on ad hoc committees and task forces of the board when appropriate;
- take on assignments when asked and when possible;
- commit to regular attendance at AHM board meetings (attendance below 50 percent is cause for dismissal from the board), prepare by reading materials in advance, participate in discussion, and exercise objective thinking in board deliberations;
- disclose and avoid conflict-of-interest situations and any appearance of conflict of interest;
- attend special board sessions when convened;
- support the museum's fund development to further sustain the organization, whenever possible, by

  - being a member of the museum;
  - providing personal charitable support by contributing to the annual fund at the highest level according to my means;
  - identifying prospective funding sources (individuals, businesses, and foundations) and facilitating meetings when appropriate;
  - recruiting friends and colleagues for museum membership;
  - supporting museum events through personal contributions, ticket purchases and/or sales, or sponsorship.

_____

Print Name

_____   _____

Signature   Date

> **Note**
> 1. This sample letter of commitment is based on the one used by the Michigan
> Museums Association (MMA), which was drafted by the author and edited to a final
> version by a committee of the MMA board.

about expectations. If board members are well informed about the organization and about the roles and responsibilities they are being asked to take on, they are much more likely to be able and willing to participate at a level that is best for the institution. If they have not been given all of the information up front, the rest of the board may be frustrated that Mr. New Board Member is not participating at the expected level, and Mr. New Board Member may be unhappy and frustrated because he is expected to do more than he thought he signed up for. Taking time to "sell" the organization and be forthright about the work involved in board membership begins the relationship on a foundation of trust and community that can only be successful in the long run.

The responsibility to inform does not end with the agreement of a potential member to join the board. It continues with the need to provide an orientation and orientation materials when new members come on board. Give them all the tools they will need to be the best board members possible. This can mean providing them with a binder containing all of the pertinent documents, similar to what was given to them when they were being courted for board membership but with greater detail. (See textbox 5.3 for a listing of recommended binder contents.) The American Association for State and Local History (AASLH) has published sets of dividers for board binders, which guide board members about their responsibilities for historical organizations. They can serve as guideposts for building a board manual that works. New board members can be oriented individually or in a group as they join. It is an opportunity to provide behind-the-scenes tours of the facility, meet key volunteers or staff, and go over and answer questions about the materials in the board binders. If there is paid staff, an orientation should be done jointly by the board president and the director. This sets a tone and makes sure that the orientation is comprehensive.

Board Responsibilities and Structure

Whether it is a working board or some combination of board types, one of the board's most important responsibilities is to develop the museum's mission, and the other is to establish policies and to ensure that the museum adheres to them and is fiscally and ethically responsible in its practices. In carrying out these mandates, members of a working board must set their day-to-day volunteer hats aside and don the hats of the leaders they have agreed to be.

Creating a mission statement is not as easy as it may seem at first glance. Bringing any group of individuals together, no matter how big, with their many ideas and opinions about what the main purpose of the museum is and what it wants to do for its visitors and its community, is a great challenge. When you take that a step further and attempt to articulate the museum's mission in, ideally, one or two sentences, the exercise can become even more difficult. The mission statement drives everything the museum does, its collections, its exhibits, its educational programs, even the merchandise it carries in its store. That is a lot of power in one or two sentences, and therefore the process can become weighted down as members of the board feel a great investment in the result. See chapter 3 for a larger discussion of the development of a mission statement.

TEXTBOX 5.2

MISSION STATEMENTS

Here are a few examples of good, concise mission statements. While they differ, each illustrates how a great deal can be said about an organization in very few words.

- *Public Museum of Grand Rapids (Michigan):* The public museum is a nonprofit educational institution whose mission is to collect, preserve, and present the natural, cultural, and social history of the region.
- *The Wilton House Museum (Richmond, Virginia):* The mission of Wilton House Museum is to preserve the circa 1753 historic house, its collections, and its environs as an example of the late colonial and early national periods in Virginia by sharing the stories of those who contributed to the history of Wilton Plantation during the first three generations of Wilton Randolphs.
- *Stephenson County Historical Society (Freeport, Illinois):* The mission of the Stephenson County Historical Society, in partnership with the Freeport Park District, is to preserve, present, and promote local and regional history.
- *Mercer Museum/Bucks County Historical Society (Doylesville, Pennsylvania):* It is the mission of the Bucks County Historical Society to cultivate among its many audiences a broad appreciation and awareness of the past, helping people find stories and meanings that both sustain them in the present and aid them in approaching the future.

For the purpose of this chapter, see textbox 5.2 for some excellent yet diverse mission statement examples.

The other critical responsibility for the board of directors is the development of policy for the museum. What kinds of policies do boards create? The board develops and approves (in partnership with the staff, if there is a staff) the museum's collections policy, the document that dictates protocols for the acquisition and deaccession of artifacts in the museum's collection.[5] The board should develop a financial policy. How does the organization deal with its money? How are funds invested, if at all? What are the checks and balances to make sure that both the museum's financial resources and those employees or volunteers who deal with those funds are protected? If the museum has a staff, there should be a personnel policy, and some organizations even create governance policies laying out exactly how the board functions and how it relates to the various parts of the museum.

In order to fulfill these responsibilities efficiently and effectively, a museum board must have a sound and reasonable structure. In other words, it must have a finite number of members and appropriate committees in place (but not too many), the functions of those committees must be clearly defined, and the length of time directors serve on the board should be established and adhered to. The board's structure is established and laid out in its bylaws, which essentially outline the functioning of the museum's governing structure. In fact, it is useful, sometimes imperative, for museum boards to have a copy of the bylaws at every board and committee meeting for reference purposes. It seems that questions consistently arise about how the board functions, and many conflicts can be resolved by simply reviewing the bylaws.

A museum's bylaws are not static. They should be revisited by the board and staff on a regular basis to ensure that they are comprehensive and continue to meet the needs of the organization. They cannot be static because museums and organizations are not static; they change over time, perhaps adding staff, perhaps finding their initial projections of board size too low or too high. For example, a very small museum in a rural community initially wrote its bylaws to include twenty-one directors on its board. It was located in the largest city in the county with a population of less than ten thousand and struggled continuously to keep a broad membership on the board representing the entire county. The museum discovered a couple of years into its existence that its board consistently had about five or six open seats. This did not look good for potential funders and simply did not make sense, so the museum amended its bylaws to account for fifteen board members—a much more reasonable size for its location and demographic.

Another example of why bylaws need to be changed over time is that many organizations, when creating initial bylaws, do everything they can to ensure that the board is always as inclusive as possible of other stakeholder organizations or communities. For example, a museum service organization laid out its board membership in a very finite way; there had to be a certain number of members from each of four or five categories, such as history, art, science, and so forth. A similar example is a county history museum that delineates specifically that it will always have a board member from each of the cities or communities in its county. While noble in its intent, such a provision can tie the hands of the board and leave it shorthanded when a position cannot be filled by a person from the specified location and must remain vacant. In each of these cases, the boards amended the bylaws to express a general intent (i.e., "The board will make every effort to represent all communities in the county") without expressly defining the board makeup.

Bylaws must serve as a living document that grows and changes as the organization grows and changes, but there is a basic recipe for what a museum's bylaws should contain. Not all bylaws are exactly the same; they must be tailored to meet the needs of each specific organization. Here is a list of articles that should make up the core of a museum's bylaws:

1. *General:* This section can include the official name of the organization, its location, and its purpose. Some organizations in this section reference a code of ethics as well; this is an excellent idea. For example, the bylaws might state, "Members of the board are expected to work in accordance with the American Association of Museums Code of Ethics." This ensures that the ethical lines are easily accessible and that there are few, if any, ambiguous questions about what is or is not ethical.

2. *Membership and dues:* This article will lay out the membership structure for the organization. Some organizations provide a detailed listing of membership categories and dues amounts, but keep in mind that every time you change either of those things, the bylaws will need to be amended, which generally requires a vote of the membership. In this case, providing a general context is probably better.

3. *Directors:* This article lays out who serves on the board, how members are elected, how long they can serve, when meetings are, and what makes up a quorum so that business can be transacted. It also lays out how the board deals with what can be difficult issues, such as removing a member from the board for excessive absences or misconduct.

4. *Officers:* This section defines who the officers are, how they are elected, and what their responsibilities are. It might also talk about a line of succession, if there is one, and definitely expresses who leads meetings and makes decisions when the president is absent, and so forth. It will also say what powers the officers have in terms of making decisions on behalf of the board, if any.

5. *Executive committee:* The board needs to outline the responsibilities and powers of the executive committee as they relate to the board as a whole. This section needs to state when they meet, how meetings are called, and who the members of the committee are—they are usually all officers with the executive director ex officio (nonvoting).

6. *Committees:* The museum must define the number of committees it has, what the standing committees are, and what they are responsible for. Most museums have a number of standing committees, such as collections, finance, exhibits, building and grounds, and perhaps strategic planning, if appropriate. This article might also delineate who serves on committees in an ex officio capacity; oftentimes this is the executive director (if there is one) or the board president. It can also talk about how committees for a one-time purpose, ad hoc committees, are established and dissolved.

7. *Staff:* If the museum has staff, it might include a section in its bylaws that defines how staff is hired and how staff interacts with the board; for example, the executive director is hired by the board and reports to the board, but other museum staff might be hired and managed by the executive director. The article might lay out a brief policy about how grievances are addressed or simply reference a personnel policy adopted by the board.

8. *Meetings:* This article outlines when and where meetings are held, how they are called, how members are notified, and, if preferred, how meetings are run—for example, "according to *Robert's Rules of Order.*" This article can also define how a board member notifies the president of an absence and how many unexcused absences are allowed before a board member is removed.

9. *Amendments:* This article provides procedures and requirements for amendment of the bylaws.

10. *Dissolution:* All bylaws for nonprofit organizations should include an article that states how the organization will disperse its assets if it must dissolve. It is important that when constructing this article, the writers are aware of state and federal laws governing the dispersion of assets of a nonprofit, including both financial assets and artifacts.

Ethics: Governance and Collections

All boards of nonprofit organizations should clearly define a policy of ethics and go to great lengths to ensure that it is read by all members of the board

THE BOARD NOTEBOOK

One tool that can help board members keep all the information they need at their fingertips is a well-designed board notebook organized into sections of relevant information for the board member and the museum. The sections and their contents might be as follows:

1. Governance
   a. Copy of the bylaws
   b. Copy of the letter of commitment
   c. List of board members and contact information
   d. List of committees and those serving on them
2. Finances
   a. Copy of the annual budget
   b. Copy of the most recent financial report
3. Collections
   a. Copy of the collections policy
   b. Copy of the ethics policy
4. Exhibits
   a. Exhibits calendar
   b. Copies of appropriate forms and policies (i.e., exhibit proposal form, procedure for proposing exhibits)
5. Public programs
   a. Program calendar
   b. Description of existing and upcoming programs
6. Publications
   a. List of publications
   b. Deadlines for publications—for example, when and to whom materials should be submitted for the museum's newsletter

The board binder should be assembled and given to the board member during an orientation with the board president and director. It is helpful to go through each element with the new member at that time. The American Association for State and Local History developed an excellent resource to help build this notebook. Its Board Orientation Organizer Kit, which includes dividers for the notebook, is available at www.aaslhnet.org/aaslhssa/ecssashop.shopping_page.

and staff and signed by each to acknowledge they have read, understood, and agreed to each of its points. All nonprofit boards have certain ethical standards to meet, such as avoiding conflict of interest and following certain procedures for conducting board business and so forth. Museums, in addition, have certain ethical responsibilities regarding their collections and exhibitions. Because they hold artifacts in the public trust, they have a strict responsibility to behave in an ethical manner in all contexts of their work. At least two national museum organizations have developed codes of ethics for use by museums of all types and sizes, the American Association of Museums and the American Association for State and Local History.

Marie Malaro, in her book *Museum Governance*, provides context for the legal definitions of what the responsibilities of trustees (board members) are. She says, "The law demands of a trustee a duty of care, a duty of loyalty, and a duty of obedience. A duty of care requires the trustee to adhere to a certain level of faithful pursuit of the purposes of the trust rather than pursuit of personal interests or the interests of nonbeneficiaries. The duty of obedience requires fidelity to the terms of the trust."[6] The governing body of a museum has an ethical responsibility to develop, approve, and oversee policies as they relate to the fiscal, personnel, and resource management of the museum, including artifact collections. Boards of directors must behave in an ethical way or run the risk of being held personally liable for any type of real or perceived malfeasance. Most boards of directors carry directors and officers liability insurance to protect the institution and its board members in case of lawsuit.[7] Board members can be sued as individuals in the context of their service on the museum's board if the board is accused of any malfeasance.

One of the most common ways small and even larger museum boards get into ethical trouble is by making decisions that result in a board member receiving personal, usually financial, gain as a result of his or her position as a member of the board. For example, many boards understand that it is important to include members of certain professions, such as an attorney, an accountant, and perhaps a contractor or buildings-and-maintenance specialist. Having those individuals on the board is not a conflict of interest in and of itself. Consider the following:

A small museum requires the services of a certified public accountant to complete its annual financial audit. One of its board members is a CPA who is very dedicated to the organization, has been a member for many years, and at times has provided pro bono services to help the organization out. A financial audit can be an expensive undertaking for an organization operating on a lean budget, so the board CPA generously offers to do the work at a 30 percent discount. The board is ecstatic about the cost savings, and the CPA board member begins his work. This is a clear conflict of interest in two ways and can lead to a great deal of trouble for the small museum. First, no board or staff member can receive monetary benefit from the organization. Second, no one can perform the audit of financial statements of an organization for which he is a board member, because as a board member he has been part of the body that approves financial statements and budgets for the museum.

The example above illustrates a real conflict of interest. The board member, if he has not yet voted on any budget approvals, can still do the work at a discounted rate, but he must first remove himself from the board of directors. It is even better if the board puts out a request for proposals to get a selection of bids for the work. If the board member is still the most reasonable choice, he will need to resign from the board before doing or being paid for the work.

It is not just real conflict of interest that is a problem for museums or other nonprofits; it is also perceived conflict of interest. Board members should be very careful that there is never any perception by the community, the membership, or anyone else that a board member is using his or her access to information for personal gain.

Perhaps one of the most important, often overlooked, and sometimes most internally controversial ethical dilemmas faced by boards relates to the artifact collection. Often board members of small historical organizations join the board of directors because they have a passionate interest in the history of the community. Because of that passion, they may collect memorabilia or antiques that would also meet the mission of the museum. For example, many people collect historic postcards—just take a look on eBay on any given day. Board members should take a number of actions to ensure there is no real or perceived conflict of interest. First, those board members who actively collect objects that meet the collecting priorities of the museum should present a statement to the board indicating the items they collect that might also be sought by the museum. Second, when they find an object that meets the museum's collecting purpose and that they wish to acquire while they are serving on the board, they should give the museum right of first refusal. In other words, instead of purchasing the object, they need to give the museum the opportunity to purchase it first. If the museum indicates it is not interested or does not have the resources to do so, then the board member can purchase the object with no real or perceived conflict of interest. Explaining to board members that they cannot collect what they want when they want can be a difficult sale. It is important to remember that everyone who agrees to serve on the museum board should be willing to put personal agendas aside and always act in the best interest of the museum.

Museum boards are responsible for approval of what comes into the collection, but perhaps even more importantly, they are responsible for approval of what is taken out—in other words, for deaccession. While deaccessioning objects is a common practice in museums, and one taken very seriously, it can be controversial to members of the public and the community. There is a perception among the public that when a museum accepts an artifact, it should be held in perpetuity by that institution. This does not account for the fact that some artifacts, despite our best efforts, deteriorate to the point of no longer being useful for exhibition, require great cost for care and preservation, and may even jeopardize the safety of other artifacts. It does not account for the storage difficulties museums find themselves in when they own 115 wood planes or forty spinning wheels or the like. And it certainly does not account for the relatively rare instances in which museums decide to change their purpose, mission, or collecting priorities. Boards, in partnership with any staff, must develop and approve a comprehensive collections policy with a section that lays out the acceptable reasons and protocols for deaccession. Once that policy is in place, it must be followed carefully.

Objects are given to museums as part of the public trust. Boards, in order to behave in an ethical manner, *must* avoid any temptation to deaccession objects with their monetary value in mind. Except for insurance and security purposes, the monetary value of an object is irrelevant. A museum cannot ethically fund its operations by selling artifacts from the collection. In fact, it is best practice, when an object is deaccessioned from the collection and sold through public auction, to use the funds raised from that sale for the acquisition of new objects or the care and conservation of existing objects only. There have been many cases over the years of museums selling pieces from their collections to help keep the doors open. This is an unethical practice. This activity has received so much attention in recent years that New York State has introduced a bill in its state assembly prohibiting the use of funds from the sale of a museum's artifacts for any expenses traditionally considered operating costs. In addition it requires collecting institutions to have a collections management policy in place and stipulates under what conditions objects can be deaccessioned.[8] In New York's case, what museum associations have been encouraging as ethical practice is becoming legal practice.

Working with Staff

While many small museums function with no paid staff, a large number have either a single staff member, usually a director or executive director, or a couple of employees. The relationship between the staff and the members of the board, as well as key volunteers who may or may not hold a board seat, can be complex, especially in very small organizations. The development of a relationship based on mutual respect is imperative when trying to sustain a small museum, and it may require time and effort for the board to get to a comfortable place with its staff, particularly when hiring staff for the first time in a museum's history. (See textbox 5.4 for the qualities the board looks for in its director.)

Often very small museums hire staff after board members, as part of a working board, have been caring for every aspect of the museum, probably for very many years. They have decided that the organization has grown to a place where it can best be served by having a museum professional there every day. Because of financial limitations, very small museums usually attract young professionals who have recently completed their graduate training. There is great passion on both sides: The board members have put great sweat equity into the museum and have very clear ideas about how it should be run. The newly hired staff member has just completed his or her education and has been taught how to do things the "right, professional way." Both bring great knowledge and skill to the organization but need to take time to recognize that fact in each other. Sometimes this sets up a conflict that must be carefully navigated in order to establish the relationship that is best for the museum. The reality is that if both take the time to find common ground, their combined passion will work in the best interest of the organization.

Case Study

A small historical society has a twenty-one-person board with many vacancies, led by a president who is part owner in a long-time family business in the community. While the president cares about the organization, he is unable to give it the attention it needs. The first newly hired director has been trained in historical research methods, museum exhibition design and development, and collections care and management. The director begins her work at the museum with very little guidance from the existing board president. When she asks questions trying to find the boundaries of her authority, he replies, "You're the director." This is the director's first full-time museum position.

The museum has had a working board for about two years, working on a fundraising campaign to raise $250,000. When the director is hired, the board members believe most of their work is done, and she is left mostly to her own devices. Some introductions are made with stakeholders in town; she is proposed for membership in the Rotary Club and so forth. So she moves along with the day-to-day operation of the museum but does not have the background in the community or the leadership experience to move the museum forward in any significant way. The museum continues at status quo, surviving but certainly not thriving.

Sometime in the next year or two, a new president takes over. She also owns a local family business, and she and her family have been extremely active civic leaders for decades, serving on the hospital board, as well as various municipal boards and commissions. She started a domestic-abuse organization in the community, and the entire family is known and respected by stakeholders throughout the community. She is extremely engaged in the work of the museum and committed to taking the institution to the next level. She views the relationship between director and board president as a partnership. She and the director speak almost daily, and she very clearly articulates that she views the director as the expert when it comes to museum functions such as the care of collections and the development of exhibitions, and the director very clearly understands the president to be the expert when it comes to knowing the community and business practices.

Together, with a reengaged board under the leadership of this president and working with the director as part of a team, the museum completes its $250,000 capital campaign, begins presenting professional-looking temporary exhibitions, increases its educational program offerings, and partners with the Smithsonian Institution Traveling Exhibition Service and Federation of State Humanities Council's Museum on Main Street project. In the meantime, together, the director and board work to maintain a small revenue stream from county government and to open up another from city government. After the accomplishments above, with a board president who takes every opportunity to talk about the museum in group settings, with customers, and at every other possible venue, the director and board president go to a city council meeting where the museum is being considered for a potentially ongoing grant for services. The night of the meeting, city workers have to bring in additional chairs because so many supporters of the museum are there, some to speak on its behalf, many as a show of support. The director and president present the case for the museum as a team, and for the first time, the museum is awarded a substantial grant from the city.

The museum's financial relationship with the city has continued for approximately ten years. If the board president and director had not brought their individual strengths and skills together, the museum would have continued to remain on the margins of the community and not have gained its role as a community resource. Developing these kinds of relationships goes beyond simple good practice; it is reflected in the AAM's Code of Ethics, which states that the members of the board of directors must "understand and fulfill their trusteeship and act corporately, not as individuals."[9] This idea can be expanded to envelop all who work with the museum—board members, staff, and volunteers. No matter the personal agendas, ideals, ambitions, or conflicts, the purpose behind every action must be the good of the organization. This can require a great deal of care and diplomacy, but there really is a single, ultimate goal: the success of the museum.

WHAT BOARD MEMBERS NEED

Board members need their directors to

- *communicate often and clearly.* While board members want the museum's director to handle the day-to-day management of the museum, they do not want to be kept in the dark. They need to have a basic understanding of the issues and concerns the director has and deals with. One way to ensure this is to set up a weekly phone call between the director and the board president, just to touch base to see if any issues need to be dealt with or to make sure the board president is apprised of the week's activities so that, if asked by another board member or community member, he or she can respond in an educated fashion.
- *be well organized.* Board members often call with requests for specific information so that they can talk to a donor or answer a question from a friend or colleague. Sometimes they simply need information to determine how they will vote on an issue that has come before the board. It is important that the director have the answer or be able to get it efficiently. For example, this means the director needs to be organized enough to have all documents for board meetings prepared and sent to the board, either via mail or e-mail, a week before the meeting so that board members have time to read and think about them. This makes for a much more efficient board meeting and more reasoned decisions.
- *be honest, even when they've made a mistake.* Everyone makes mistakes or errors in judgment. The board wants, and needs, to be aware of these errors, big and small, to protect the director, themselves, and the organization. On the flip side, the board needs to create an environment in which the director feels able to bring these issues to the board without fear of losing his or her job (except, of course, in cases of criminal negligence, etc.)
- *be excellent listeners and deal with both board members and members of the community with respect and diplomacy.* One of the greatest lessons a young director can learn is to understand that everyone brings something to the table, and all should work for the good of the museum. Board members want and need directors to hear their ideas and listen to their visions. Directors bring museum expertise, but board members offer talents that directors may not yet possess. Seeing themselves and board members as part of the same team is critical to success.

Conclusion

The country is filled with small museums that house, preserve, and share the history and culture of their communities. They do it because they are passionate and because they believe to their core that if they do not, no one else will, and the things that represent the community's history will be gone forever. There is probably some truth to that belief. Preserving this heritage goes beyond making sure the artifacts are safe and exhibited appropriately. Having a strong governing structure, with a diversified board and strong leadership is the bedrock for the ultimate mission of the museum. Without an understanding of the mechanisms through which boards must work and diligence in developing appropriate policies and making sure they are carried out, the museum cannot possibly carry out its mission of preservation and education. This lack puts everything it desires at risk. The beautiful part of this problem is that the solution is ultimately pretty simple. Many, many resources available to small boards will answer questions that arise and help them develop an appropriate infrastructure and navigate pitfalls along the way. Small museums are part of the larger museum community and therefore a part of the exchange of ideas.

Resource List

A plethora of available materials talk about governance, its various models, and how to achieve successful governance. The following selections are particularly useful for small organizations, and some are specifically focused on museum governance.

Books
Ingram, Richard T. *Ten Basic Responsibilities of Nonprofit Boards.* Washington, DC: BoardSource, 2009.
Malaro, Marie C. *Museum Governance.* Washington, DC: Smithsonian Institution Press, 1994

Organizations and Websites
American Association for State and Local History (www.aaslh.org): As mentioned in the chapter, AASLH developed a useful and affordable board tool kit. It provides dividers for board notebooks that have printed material about the corresponding topic (i.e., a policy of ethics as it relates to collections management). You will find the kit listed at www.aaslhnet.org/aaslhssa/ecssashop.shopping_page.

BoardSource (www.boardsource.org): BoardSource provides many publications and question-and-answer leaflets that are invaluable to all organizations, small and large. The Q&A section of the website is particularly helpful because each item deals with a very specific issue or question common to all boards. Click on the "Knowledge Center" button at the top of the home page to find the Q&As. BoardSource's list of publications is also very helpful.

Museum Trustees Association (www.mta-hq.org): The Museum Trustees Association is helpful because it deals specifically with the needs of museum trustees or board members. The association provides an excellent bibliography of literature related to governance.

Notes

1. Marie C. Malaro, *Museum Governance* (Washington, DC: Smithsonian Institution Press, 1994), vii.

2. *Oxford English Dictionary*, online, entry number 1 for "governance."

3. *Note:* The board did hire a fundraising consultant for this work. The consultant helped them organize into a useful fundraising structure and provided them with excellent development training (i.e., in how to "make the ask"). Members of the board did most of the actual fundraising, however.

4. This statement was developed by Phil Porter, director of the Mackinac State Historic Parks and president of the Michigan Museums Association at the time. Slight changes have been made here to provide a more generic example.

5. To "deaccession" an object means officially to remove it from the museum's permanent artifact collection.

6. Malaro, *Museum Governance*, 9.

7. See www.prismnet.com/~tam/Membership/doeo.html. This is the Texas Association of Museums Directors & Officers program, but it lays out the parameters of coverage as an example.

8. New York State Assembly Bill A06959A; also referenced in Robin Pogrebin, "Bill Seeks to Regulate Museums' Art Sales," *New York Times*, March 17, 2009. Also the American Association for State and Local History (AASLH) ethics policy can be found at "Statement of Professional Standards and Ethics," AASLH, www.aaslh.org/ethics.htm.

9. See "Code of Ethics for Museums," American Association of Museums, www.aam-us.org/museumresources/ethics/coe.cfm.

MARRY ME! THE RELATIONSHIP BETWEEN THE DIRECTOR AND THE BOARD

Katie Anderson

T he relationship between the director and the board of a small museum is
akin to a marriage. As with a marriage, you have a choice to make before
you take a position at a museum, so choose wisely! It takes effort on both
sides. It is not always roses and champagne. As in a marriage, communication is
everything in the relationship between the director and the board.

Being a small museum director may be the most rewarding and challenging position within the museum field. For many museum professionals whose
interests are generalized, it can be a healthy fit. Often, however, new directors
think being in a small museum means they will be able to enjoy the varied responsibilities of designing exhibitions, creating educational programming, and
caring for collections exclusively. They are probably in for a rude awakening.
Depending on the structure of the board-director relationship and the available
resources, the director may be expected to perform all or most of the fundraising, marketing, volunteer recruitment and management, and financial reporting.
In addition to these tasks, the director must build relationships with each board
member while helping to shape the development of the overall board. Building
these relationships means spending a lot of time talking and listening to better
understand the board members. It also means helping them better understand
the operations of the museum.

One of the most challenging tasks for first-time directors (and even for
experienced directors at new organizations) is determining the boundaries of
responsibility and authority; this can vary greatly from museum to museum. It
is particularly useful to ask probing questions during the interview process to
determine what expectations the board has for the director. Delegation of authority and distinction of roles are discussed later in this chapter.

In the best-case scenario, the rewards far outweigh the stress of carrying the
weight of the organization on your shoulders. Sharing the load helps. This is
where the board comes in. Its members are your partners, but collectively they
are also your boss. You should share the same general goals for the museum,
but you probably come from vastly different perspectives. You have the museum

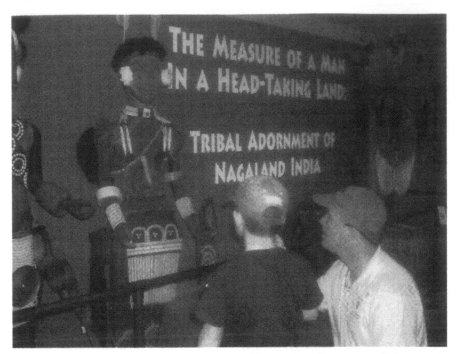

Photo 6.1. Guests enjoy a temporary exhibit on the adornment of the people of Nagaland, India, at the Bead Museum in Glendale, Arizona. (Photo by Katie Anderson)

training and experience; you are the professional. They are the volunteer board members who probably have no museum training or experience but definitely have strong opinions about what you should be doing. They probably care deeply for the museum and are burdened with the fiduciary responsibility for it. While you may leave the museum at some point in your career and move on, they may have a lifetime commitment to it.

If you do not already know, find out why the board members are involved with the museum and what their backgrounds are. This will help you understand their motivations and how they can be of assistance to you. Having a diverse board refers to more than demographics. It is important to have people versed in the following areas if possible: marketing, retail (if you have a store), law, finance, construction, and education, among others. Their expertise and skills are resources that you will need to utilize.

While it may be tempting to show off your knowledge and expertise by pointing out problems, resist the urge (or at least be diplomatic). Rather than increase their confidence in you, it could come across as adversarial. At one of my museums, I suggested changing some exhibit panels that had been created ten years previously by volunteers. They were tattered, and I was eager to show what I could do. Though I was tactful, several board members, including the founder, were against it. They were proud of what the volunteers had done and somewhat defensive regarding any criticism. A year later, during a community meeting about the museum, we learned that many people felt the exhibits should be done more professionally. The same board members who had disagreed with me before now thought it was a wonderful idea to make the changes. They needed to hear it from the community members. Sometimes you have to promote and communicate desired changes through other people.

What Are the Roles of the Governing Board for a Small Museum?

The overall role of the board is to strategically guide the museum forward. Whether it is in relation to finances, programming, or staffing, the board must look at the big picture and pull all the various elements together into a cohesive vision and plan. The following list of board tasks is adapted from a book I highly recommend, Robert C. Andringa and Ted W. Engstrom's *Nonprofit Board Answer Book: Practical Guide for Board Members and Chief Executives.*

- Determining and clarifying the museum's mission
- Selecting, supporting, and evaluating the director
- Ensuring effective strategic planning
- Ensuring and managing sufficient resources
- Developing the museum's standing and role in the community
- Guaranteeing legal and ethical integrity
- Recruiting, orienting, and evaluating board members

First and foremost, the governing board determines the museum's mission. Why does the museum exist? Whom does it serve and how? Is there a need for this service? Is another organization filling this need better, or is this museum truly needed? In today's harsh economic climate, being relevant to your community, however you define it, is necessary for survival.

The museum's mission is the fundamental reason for its existence. It should not change on a whim but should be regularly challenged and explored in order to keep the museum relevant to the community it serves. As existing or potential programs are explored, asking whether they meet the mission is crucial. In the best-case scenario, the board will work with the director to determine which programs best meet the mission and are therefore appropriately supportable.

The board is also responsible for selecting, supporting, and evaluating the director. Too often boards of small museums hire a director and think their work is done in this area. Far from it. The board and director must continually work together to strengthen their relationship. Once the board selects a director it feels is a good match, it must support the decisions of the director in order for the museum to succeed. Challenges to these decisions must be made in an appropriate setting, never in front of other staff or visitors. A personal conversation with the director to understand the decision is the best place to start.

The board must assess the performance of the director on a regular basis. He or she should not be surprised during an evaluation to hear either praise or concerns. These should be addressed as they happen. As with any other employee, receiving constructive feedback from the board throughout the year will enhance the director's performance. Then a formal, annual performance evaluation becomes less threatening and more helpful. Board members may feel that a performance evaluation is not urgent if a merit or cost-of-living increase is not going to be offered. But regardless of the financial situation, the board should communicate with the director about his or her performance at least annually so that any course corrections can be set in motion.

Along with determining the museum's mission, the board is responsible for ensuring effective strategic planning. I highly recommend bringing in a third-party facilitator to help conduct your planning session. A multiyear plan can take half a day or longer with the board after tremendous preparation by the director. Since the director has a deeper understanding of the operation of the museum, he or she should prepare topics to be considered at this guided session. Strategic planning is not usually about reinventing the museum. It is about responding to changing community needs and planning how to secure resources to meet them.

It is the board's responsibility to ensure and manage sufficient resources to meet the needs of the museum. Yes, this means fundraising or at least participating in a development program! Board members must be willing to assist with development. This does not mean they have to write big checks. Your board should collectively decide on the annual gift commitment level. But its members have to be a part of the overall development plan in your museum.

Introducing their friends to the museum with a special reception and behind-the-scenes tour is a great way to ease hesitant board members into the development process. They do not all have to be able to ask for money, but they need to get their friends excited about the museum. Do not accept a comment like "But my friends don't have money" without responding. When you hear this, reassure board members that their networks are broader than they think. Bringing in their friends and getting them excited about the museum will have a ripple effect. If nothing else, it will increase awareness and enthusiasm in the community.

Most people do not like to ask for money because they do not know how. I used to think I was being pushy to ask for money directly. I had to shift the way I thought about it. By not asking, I was making the decision for the prospective donor. I took a course on nonprofit fundraising that helped me rethink my feelings on making "the ask." Then I was able to be more helpful to board members who were struggling with the same issues.

Ensuring resources should also include in-kind gifts, such as

- furniture, office supplies, and equipment;
- bookkeeping services and marketing services;
- shared facilities or subsidized rents;
- shared advertising and free radio spots;
- donated or subsidized refreshments for events.

Another important resource for a small museum is a strong volunteer base. Board members can help grow that base through networking. Some find asking people to volunteer less threatening than asking for money. Yet, in my experience, volunteers provide significant financial support through memberships, gift shop sales, and donations, as well as by providing unpaid staffing that can save many thousands of dollars each year. While the board can play a big role in recruiting volunteers, it should not be involved in managing the volunteer staff. Volunteers should be considered unpaid staff and therefore report to the director, not the board.

Managing the resources includes budgeting, determining the best way to grow an endowment, and the like. Should funds be held all in one bank or spread across several? How should unrestricted cash gifts be used? Should gifts of stock or property be sold and converted to cash immediately? If so, how will that be managed? These are all questions for the board to wrestle with.

Everyone involved with a small museum should be involved in public relations. In particular, it is a role of the board to develop the museum's standing and role in the community. To be clear, the director, unless otherwise stated in the bylaws or a job description, should be the main spokesperson for the museum. It is important to present a consistent message to the public. But everyone can act as an ambassador, sharing what the museum means to them and inviting new people to visit and join.

A governing board has a tremendous fiduciary responsibility for the operations of the museum and to guarantee legal and ethical integrity. Board members can be sued if they are perceived to be conducting business in an illegal or unethical manner. This serious responsibility is not to be entered into lightly. If your museum has not adopted a code of ethics, you should consider drafting one. These remind the board members of their duties and are helpful, if not mandatory, when applying for grants from certain governmental agencies. The American Association of Museums (AAM) and the small museum list serve (see the resources at the end of this chapter) are resources for locating a sample code of ethics.

Photo 6.2.   A West African stilt walker amazes crowds at the International Family Fun Day at the Bead Museum in Glendale, Arizona. (Photo by Katie Anderson)

Delegation of Authority

Authority for the day-to-day operations should be delegated by the board to the director in formal documentation, such as the bylaws, the formally approved job description, or a staff handbook. The latter is helpful in communicating this authority to all of the staff who need to understand and follow the chain of command. The AAM document on the Accreditation Commission's Expectations Regarding Delegation of Authority dated December 17, 2004, states that the commission requires an accredited museum to have a full-time director with museum experience who is "delegated authority for the day-to-day operations of the museum and allocated resources sufficient to operate the museum effectively. Functionally, this position is the chief executive officer with responsibilities including, but not limited to, hiring and firing staff, executing the budget, implementing policies, and managing programs and staff."

The clear delegation of authority supports the distinction of the governance roles of the board from the management roles of the director. This clarity promotes communication and collaboration while reducing duplication of effort. It is presumed that the governing board has hired a director with the expertise to run the museum and therefore should be allowed to do so without interference.

With the authority to act independently regarding day-to-day operations, the director is able to achieve more. Resources, including time, are better spent. Conversely, the board is able to focus on steering the museum through determining the mission, setting policies, ensuring the bylaws are followed, approving the budget, creating strategic plans, establishing financial controls, and ensuring that adequate resources are procured to advance the museum's mission.

What's in a Name?

Your title can mean a great deal. It can tell the community your role and level of authority.

- If you will be dealing often with corporate leaders, the title of president and/or chief executive officer (CEO) will allow them to understand your responsibilities and authority within the organization. In this situation, the head of the board of directors or trustees should be called the chair rather than the president. All of this assumes that this individual has the authority to make binding executive decisions for the museum.
- The more traditional title of executive director is given to the top executive of a museum. In the nonprofit world, it is widely understood as the equivalent of CEO.
- Titles that may be used to indicate the principal operational person, if not executive, include

  - museum director
  - director
  - director or curator
  - site manager

Names also matter in an advisory group. The term *advisory board* rolls easily off the tongue. But it may be misconstrued as a group with voting power. Try advisory council or committee for a group of individuals who offer expertise to the museum. You may also have a group of influential community members who become ambassadors for the museum. Their main goal is to promote the museum through their network.

Is a Board Member a Volunteer?

Since board members volunteer their time, what is the difference between their roles as board member and as volunteer? This is one of the trickiest areas for small museum administrators to navigate. The board members must understand

Table 6.1. Governance vs. Volunteer Role

Governance Role	Volunteer Role
• Voting at board meetings	• Helping to install an exhibit
• Recruiting new board members	• Working in the store
• Evaluating the director	• Setting up for an event
• Reading and analyzing operational and financial reports	• Selling raffle tickets or participating in a phone bank
• Sitting on a Collections Committee that determines what to accession	• Working with staff to process accessions to the collection

the difference between their governance role and any additional volunteer activity they undertake. Typically, the director will need to help clarify. Table 6.1 contains examples of the different activities in governing versus volunteer roles.

As a volunteer, a board member should take direction from the director or staff person who is organizing the project. Staff members understand the daily operations and are best suited to direct activities. Many times when board members work closely with staff in a volunteer capacity, they try to take a leadership role and run the program. They may even try to have the staff member report directly to them. The best way to thwart this is to provide guidelines before the event. You may want to explain, "Mary planned the event and knows what is going on, so she is the lead and will give you instructions." Encourage board members to come straight to you if they have any concerns or suggestions rather than trying to redirect things on their own. Be sure to start and end this conversation with a generous dose of gratitude.

It can be tricky to maintain boundaries between staff and board members when you have a very hands-on board, as many small museums do. It is easy for the staff to become comfortable with a board member if they are working on a project together. But the director must make it clear to staff and board members alike that the staff member should not introduce new ideas or problems to a board member without discussing them with the director first. As the director, you should have the opportunity to formulate your message about the issue before it comes to the attention of a board member. A staff member who continues to discuss issues with a board member could unintentionally create a rift between the director and the board member.

The President

Though technically the director reports to the board rather than an individual, it is very likely that the president or chair of the board will have the most contact with the director. It is vital that you create a strong bond with this person if at all possible. The president can have a tremendous influence on the rest of the board in deciding what areas of programming to keep or cut, making policy changes, and determining how best to meet budgetary needs, including possibly cutting staff or programs. Although you want the entire board to understand your role as director, it is most important that the president and vice president do so in order that they may influence others.

A president who does not understand her role or the director's can inadvertently create confusion about the delegation of authority and the distinction of roles. Conversely, a strong and respectful president can lead the museum through a crisis or help it grow during better times. A strong president will step in when other board members are trying to assert themselves on the operational side and will support the decisions of the director. Other attributes of a strong president include having a passion for the museum, being a vigorous ambassador for the museum, having a strong business sense, and being open to learning about museum standards and operations.

Tips for Success

First-Time Directors

The board members are your allies, not your friends. Do not succumb to the temptation to tell them all the problems you are having with staff or in adjusting to the new position. If you are not ready to act on a problem, do not talk about it with a board member. Focus on sharing successes. But do not let a problem fester.

Table 6.2. Tips for Success

	Tips for	
First-Time Directors	Managing Your Relationship with the Board	Managing Museum Performance
• Don't treat board members like friends.	• Meet informally with board members regularly.	• Provide an Annual Operations Plan to the board.
• Offer solutions when discussing problems.	• Track board participation in board meetings and museum functions.	• Create and monitor individual work plans for key staff and yourself.
• Don't go to a board meeting unprepared.	• Track communication with board members.	• Make sure the financial reporting is in order.
• Build alliances with local cultural organizations.	• Use consultants to say what you need to say about contentious topics.	• Utilize performance benchmarking and enhancement programs.
• Don't be afraid of performance reviews.	• Use local resources to provide board training.	
• Ask that the board review their own performance.	• Help recruit new board members.	
• Identify the museum's biggest challenges.		
• Find a healthy work/life balance.		

125

When you must share problems with the board, be sure to offer solutions. More specifically, offer the solution you want to see happen. This will go a long way in building their confidence in your abilities. By thinking through the problem ahead of time and determining an appropriate solution, you can avoid having to implement less effective solutions that others may suggest. After presenting your solution, be open to hearing other solutions that may be more effective.

Do not go into a board meeting without a fairly clear idea of what is likely to transpire. Among the board members, you will undoubtedly have several close allies. Make sure you talk to each of these people before the board meeting regarding any decisions that must be made. Encourage them to sway other members beforehand. The board meeting is not the time for surprises, especially when they can be avoided.

If you are moving to a new town, make immediate contact with the other museums, art organizations, and historical societies in the area. Their leaders can become your allies as well. One of the great things about working for a nonprofit is that even when we compete for people's leisure time and contributions, we still are willing to help each other. So take advantage of the knowledge and skills of your colleagues. It can be lonely working in a small museum. But be careful what you share about your museum and board until you know the interconnectedness of the people involved. This is particularly necessary in a small town where civic leaders may participate in more than one organization.

Performance reviews should have two parts—a self-assessment done by the director and an assessment of the director done by the board. The self-assessment is an important opportunity for you to communicate your successes. It is also the time for you to look honestly at areas that need improvement. The board may be able to help with resources for professional development. Ideally, the self-assessment is presented to the board before it finishes its assessment. Your honest assessment can help the board prepare an appropriate appraisal of its own. It is imperative that you know what the board really thinks of your work if you want your tenure to be long.

It is equally important that the board review its own performance, as individuals and as a unit. This is rarely done consistently. Most boards only evaluate themselves as part of a specific program, like AAM's Museum Assessment Program (MAP). Board performance is critical to the health of a museum. The decisions made by the board affect the museum in the short and long term. The level of dysfunction in a board will affect morale, possibly leading to the resignation of high-performing but frustrated staff and board members. Board training can help, but it should be combined with a more consistent approach. Putting an item on the agenda for each board meeting that focuses on how to improve the board provides ongoing opportunities for open discussions. Sometimes a standing committee called a board development committee is used to recruit and nominate new members. This committee should also be responsible for the evaluative process that leads to true development.

Quickly identify the museum's most important challenges from the perspective of the staff (volunteer or paid) and the board. Do they match? Are the challenges internal, such as staff morale, a budget crisis, or slipping attendance? Or are there external challenges, like a recession, unemployment, or changes in the community? Look for ways to turn the challenges into opportunities. What particular issues does your community face that the museum may be able to address? Can you partner with a local library to help increase literacy? Can you partner with a local historical industry that is trying to revive interest in a dying craft to create jobs?

Treat yourself well. It is easy to become completely absorbed in this work. But to do your best work, you need to have a balanced life. Many of us simply do not think about the things we can do to take care of ourselves. Making a list and keeping it handy might trigger you to pick up the phone and make an appointment for a massage!

Managing Your Relationship with the Board

Meet individually with your board members for coffee or lunch on a regular basis. An informal setting creates a relaxed environment. Getting to know your board members helps you understand their motivations for involvement with the museum. You can also determine how risk averse and fiscally conservative they are and how they feel about particular programs. It can be helpful to learn their perspective before voicing your opinion so you can craft your response. Once you determine which board members are your strongest allies, set up a schedule that allows you to meet with them more frequently than with other board members if the board is large. You should meet with these allies before a board meeting at which a vote is required, particularly on a contentious issue.

Use tools such as paper forms, Excel, Outlook, or PastPerfect to track board participation in board meetings and museum functions. This information is helpful in evaluating board performance. If board members are not participating in events or meetings, how exactly are they contributing? Is there a more productive person who could fill that seat on the board?

Use tools to track your communication with board members. It bears repeating that communication is everything. Knowing what you have told people and what issues they have expressed concern about to you is critical. Communication tracking logs can be found in planning calendars like Franklin Covey, or you can create a simple spreadsheet. Think about what it makes sense for you to track and make your system work for you. Some tracking fields to

Table 6.3. Board of Directors Application and Information

Board of Directors Application

As mentioned previously, tools can help you manage your board relationships. Creating forms to track information can be of tremendous help. As part of the recruitment process, a prospective board member could complete an application. The application would include the following:

- Contact information—personal and business
- Birthday (month/day)
- Preferred method of communication (phone, cell, email, fax)
- Areas of expertise and how they would envision assisting the museum
- Check boxes for committee selection—include a note indicating that all board members must serve on at least one committee
- Signature of prospective board member and date

Additional Board Member Information

It is useful to have an information sheet on each board member to track their participation and contributions to the museum. Whereas the application is completed by the board member, the information sheet is completed by the director for his/her own use and is not shared with the board. Consider these fields:

- Basic information—contact information, profession, spouse's name, other family members, email, birthday
- Term beginning and end dates—is it renewable?
- Important community ties
- Reason for joining the board
- Table to track donations—include description (cash, in-kind, service), date received, date acknowledged by the director
- Museum events attended
- Volunteer service for the museum—include dates, number of hours, type of work
- Absences from board meeting

This information is vital in managing your relationship with each board member. Keeping it on a single form allows quick access and analysis.

consider are date of conversation, name, main topic, decisions made, questions left unanswered, concerns raised, and follow-up required. Such tracking will help you judge whether you need to spend more time communicating with various board members.

Consultants are often not within the budgetary constraints of small museums. However, you may be able to find another museum professional willing to trade services with you. Having an outside expert strengthens your message. So use consultants to say what you need to say about sensitive topics that the board finds contentious.

Use local resources such as the following to provide board training, but do it with a specific end in mind:

- Find a nonprofit leader to facilitate a board retreat to develop a strategic plan.
- Ask a board member to accompany you to the annual AAM and AASLH meetings to participate in specific sessions that address your immediate concerns for the museum.
- Ask a board member to join you for training at a local university before your retreat to develop a strategic plan.

The director should help recruit new board members. To do this, you need to be involved in the community. Getting involved with a civic organization can give you an outlet to help with work-life balance while also helping you get to know people in the community who might be candidates for the board. Who would not love the opportunity to hire their own boss?

Managing Museum Performance

The performance of a museum relies heavily on a thorough, well-thought-out plan. The plan should include a multiyear perspective as well as an annual plan that can be broken down into manageable tasks for the staff to implement. While the board is more active in developing the multiyear strategic plan, the director should provide an annual operations plan based on the board-approved multiyear plan.

A three- to five-year strategic plan, aside from being necessary for many grant applications, is a tool to keep everyone working toward the same goals. An annual operations plan presents the director's plan for adhering to the multiyear strategic plan within a given year. The operations plan is much more action oriented and detailed. It should address all the key areas of the director's responsibilities: finances and development, exhibits and programs, personnel, marketing, community engagement, and the like. The plan should state goals, specific actions, time frames for the actions, and resources needed.

From this plan, you can create individual work plans for key staff and yourself. These work plans should include goal, activity, outcome, to-do list, time line, resources needed, and performance evaluation. This is a working document that should be monitored by the employee and director regularly. The work plan should tie into the annual operations plan, which is based on the board-approved strategic plan, thereby providing a tool that brings the big picture of the strategic plan down to the level of frontline staff. It also promotes accountability by providing clear tracking of performance (see table 6.4).

Table 6.4. Employee Work Plan (by Katie Anderson)

EMPLOYEE WORKPLAN

The _____ Museum — Development Director

July 2008–December 2008

Goal	Activity "What We Do"	Outcome "So What?"	Tactics "To Do List"	Timeline	Anticipated Inputs "Resources Needed"	Performance Credit
Insert goal from operations plan.	Insert name of the activity. There could be more than one activity for each goal.	Insert outcome from logic model.	Insert list of tactics to complete goal. This also serves as a roadmap for others to follow if necessary.	Insert date(s) to be completed.	Insert any resource needed to accomplish goal/activity. This could be personnel, office supplies, meeting space, and so forth.	This section is used by supervisor to score to support performance reviews.
Enhance fundraising activities to meet annual budgetary needs	Maintain 100 percent giving by the board	Meet income goal of $129K for donations revenue Maintains strong commitment to the museum from board members	• Develop Founder's Day • Personal call and/or meeting with each board member • Monthly update via e-mail to board members • Include board recognition in newsletter and on website • Include board in Red Book	• September 2008 • August 2008 • ongoing • ongoing • August 2008 or January 2009	• Meeting space • Sponsor/underwriter • Nomination to Red Book	Raised $130,000
	Enhance annual campaign to $10K	Meet income goal of $129K for donations revenue	• Develop "Case for Support" • Direct mail piece • Host "open house" • Include campaign materials with admission purchase	• August 2008 • October 2008 • September 2008 • August/September		Draft completed

BEFORE YOU COMMIT

It is prudent to ask many questions about the role of the board and what it expects of the director during the interviewing process. This may help you avoid a mismatch of your skills and board members' expectations. Remember that you are interviewing them as well. Here are some sample questions:

- What is your current budget? How long have you been able to maintain that level of funding? How is your funding diversified? Who is responsible for fundraising? What do you see as the board's role in fundraising?
- What role does the board play in managing staff?
- Can you recite or paraphrase the mission of the museum? (This will tell you how engaged they are.)
- Do you have a copy of the bylaws and annual report? (If they have trouble producing them, this indicates, at the very least, that they are not organized.)
- What do you see as the museum's biggest challenge?
- Does the museum have a strategic plan?
- What is your process for evaluating the director? How often does this happen?
- Does the director have full authority to hire and fire?
- How does the board deal with potential conflicts of interest?

You should always research a prospective employer. You can research museums using the GuideStar website (www.guidestar.com), which is designed to provide information about registered nonprofits throughout the United States to potential donors. If the museum filed a tax return, you should find a PDF of the actual filing with the IRS on GuideStar's site. A tax return can provide helpful information about the financial stability of the organization. One drawback is that the information is usually at least six months old as it is only posted after the taxes for the prior year are filed.

It is vital to know yourself in order to find a good fit. Ask yourself a few questions before you interview.

- Do you like to manage people or projects? What is your management style? If the board is very hands-on, will you be able work with it?

(continued)

- What new skills do you hope to gain from the position? Can the people on the board help you gain the experience you are looking for? Are the challenges going to stretch you and help you grow?
- What work/life balance are you looking for? Will this position require too much of your time? Fifty- to sixty-hour workweeks are common for small museum directors.
- Do you like research, collections management, and exhibitions but not the other aspects of museum work?
- Where do you want to live? If this position would require a move, do you really want to uproot? What are the financial implications? It could take a long time to recover financially, even if the museum is willing to help with expenses.
- Do you need a network of colleagues? It can be very lonely in a small town as one of a small handful of museum professionals.
- How long do you think you could be happy in that town, at that museum?

Financial planning is vital to a museum's performance and can only happen when reliable information is available. Make sure the financial reporting is in order and that you understand how to read it so that you can explain it to any board members who may need help. Also, review a budget-to-actual report monthly. Do not let finances surprise you or your board. If the financial situation is dire, make sure the board understands the seriousness of the situation. Work closely with it on a recovery plan. If the reports continue to be dire, you may need to be the one to introduce the idea of closing the museum or merging with another. Of course this topic could fill a chapter or an entire book in itself. But it is important for you to recognize that you know more about the operations than anyone, and your leadership is vital during crises. Do not be afraid to introduce painful topics. However, you should prepare before doing so. How you present a message directly affects how it is received.

Performance can be greatly enhanced with help from outside resources. Utilize programs like AAM's MAP or the AASLH's Standards and Excellence Program for History Organizations (you do not have to be a history museum to find it useful). These tried-and-true programs were developed by experts in museums of all shapes and sizes. Take advantage of them to help you and your board focus, set performance benchmarks, and enhance programs.

Stories from the Field

In my experience, one of the best ways to expand our thoughts on a particular situation is to hear from others in similar situations. Museum professionals are typically very willing to talk to others about their challenges and how they overcame them. You may find some helpful ideas in the following case studies, even if these situations do not exactly reflect your own.

Case Study 1

Glen Kyle is managing director of a small local history museum in northeastern Georgia. He became director in September 2007 and was still incumbent when this was written. The museum had been around for fifteen to twenty years in different guises. It moved into a new building and changed its name in 2004.

With an annual budget of $200,000, the museum has one part-time and two full-time paid staff members whose salaries comprise roughly 45 percent of the annual budget. Kyle directs the full-time education coordinator/volunteer supervisor/administrative assistant and the part-time bookkeeper. He is fortunate to have around one hundred volunteers. He plans to hire another part-time person to take on the administrative assistant duties so that the other full-time person can focus on education and volunteers.

Kyle says, "We have bylaws and standing board policies in place, and an executive committee (EC) that does a lot of the 'foot work' for operations; as a matter of fact, we are still trying to iron out exactly how the EC and the full board interact, and what that relationship really should be. Our small size means the board members are very involved as volunteers, which makes them 'my boss' when we're in a board meeting, but I'm 'their boss' when they are serving as volunteers at the front desk, at an event, as docents, etc." Through attrition the board is trying to reduce gradually to the minimum number of board members.

As for board giving requirements, only membership in the organization is required, and the minimum level for that is $35. However, members currently run the gamut from $35 individual memberships to the highest level at $5,000. Term limits do not exist, though they are desired by the managing director.

Kyle describes his board as "very even on gender representation, but lack[ing] ethnic diversity. We're also heavily weighted towards retirement age,

Table 6.5.   Case Study 1—Key Facts

Institution and Location: Northeast Georgia History Center, Gainesville, Georgia
Administrator: Glen Kyle, Managing Director

Type of Governance	Private 501(c)(3)		
Budget	$200,000	**Founded**	~1990
Staff Size	2 FT + 1 PT	**Size of Board**	32–41

Table 6.6. Case Study 1—Tips

Glen Kyle's Tips for Improving Board Relations
1. Remain cordial and available. Listen to them all, even if you disagree with their position. This takes a lot of time but is worth the effort.
2. Spend time thinking about and anticipating the needs and concerns of individual board members. Address them before they become an issue or come up in a board meeting.
3. Bring in some "other authority" to back up your ideas, whether it is a consultant, professional texts, or research articles.
4. Work with officers to make sure you get a president whom you can work with. Having a new boss every year is bad enough, but having one whom you don't see eye to eye with can be a disaster for you, the board, and the institution as a whole.

but we do have five younger (family-age) members, and the board mostly recognizes that the average age needs to decrease. We have a pretty broad experience base on the board, but not much of it in nonprofits and none in terms of museum professionals (excluding the work they've done here)."

One of the biggest challenges the board has faced is giving up authority to the managing director. Kyle states, "Some are handling it better than others. As with many museums, the board has been representative of the more affluent, retired crowd, and as such they have a hard time realizing that there are larger audiences out there. In a nutshell, I think the biggest challenge has been 'becoming a real museum under the guidance of a real museum professional.' The board, as a body, has generally been very supportive. Individually, as you can guess, it varies depending upon that individual's personal set of priorities and resistance to change." Kyle has gradually been able to gain the board's confidence so that members feel comfortable sharing responsibility for the institution with him. With open communication, they are all becoming clearer on the role the board plays versus the role of the managing director.

Fundraising is a key role for any board. Kyle feels that fundraising is not his strong suit and that the board is not as engaged as it should be. Several members of the board give at significant levels, and they feel that is the limit of their responsibility as far as fundraising. Two or three people on the board help with any and all fundraising efforts for the year. The rest acknowledge that it is a responsibility but do not actively engage in the efforts. This is not uncommon.

Case Study 2

Kelli Pickard is museum director of the Log Cabin Village, which is run by the city of Forth Worth, Texas. As a municipal museum, it does not have a governing board but rather city management, which the director reports to. She has been director for twelve years and has found that education and communication are the keys for interacting with city management. The museum has four full-time

Table 6.7. Case Study 2—Key Facts

Institution and Location: Log Cabin Village, Fort Worth, Texas
Administrator: Kelli Pickard, Museum Director

Type of Governance	Municipal (City)		
Budget	$400,000	Founded	~1965
Staff Size	4 FT + 11 PT	Size of Board	n/a

staff: Pickard, a curator, an educator, and a maintenance person. Four part-time staff run the gift shop, and seven part-time interpreters work in the village.

A common challenge of any board is that members might not understand exactly what it takes to run a museum. In a city government, this can be extremely challenging, as the main focus is the overall operation of a municipality, not the daily management of a museum or other specific facility. Pickard has a support group, which has a board. This increases the number of people she has to keep in touch with to make sure they understand the needs and challenges of the museum.

Approaching city management with problems that require assistance could seem cumbersome because the individuals do not always understand the operations. Pickard has found that frequent communication helps keep everyone in

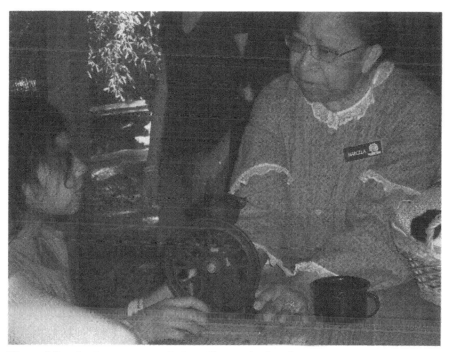

Photo 6.3. An interpreter grinds coffee at the hands-on cabin at the Log Cabin Village in Fort Worth, Texas. (Photo by Kelli Pickard)

the loop and eliminates the stress brought on by surprise situations. She presents a monthly report containing information on which groups or potential supporters she has spoken to, what events were held, how the museum was represented to the public, any marketing efforts, meetings attended, and training attended by staff. This is not only a great tool for keeping the city management informed but also a helpful historical document for Pickard to keep.

According to Pickard, the most important aspect of working in a larger system is learning the system itself. How do you function within it? How can you use it to benefit the museum? How is the museum valued within this system? What aspects of the system are larger than you and must be accepted rather than changed? What is worth challenging, and do you have the support to be successful?

A support group was founded a year after Pickard became the director. This private 501(c)(3) organization's sole purpose, as stated in its bylaws, is to support the Log Cabin Village in the city parks department. The foundation raises money to support programming and has helped with matching grants that have supported conservation work and professional development. It is important for the support group to understand the museum, and Pickard communicates with its members regularly. The support group is not involved in day-to-day operations of the Log Cabin Village. It exists to provide funding and to advocate in the community for the organization.

Overall communication has been a recurring theme for Pickard. The city supervisor conducts weekly staff meetings, which provide an opportunity for Pickard to visit department managers as a group and one-on-one if necessary. She keeps staff informed of city issues so they can have a broader perspective. She meets regularly with the support group as well. Pickard says that the biggest glitches she has faced have been when there was not enough communication. Major breakdowns can happen.

Educating managers, staff, and board members is also important. At a prior museum with a traditional board, Pickard had a board member show up for an exhibit opening. Pickard was the only full-time staff member and had a part-time receptionist. She was responsible for everything, including researching, designing, and building the exhibit. After the opening, the board member said she had been expecting more. Pickard's heart sank, but she took the opportunity to educate the board member rather than let the relationship be ruined by hard feelings. She explained that she literally had to construct pieces of the exhibit. She invited the board member to help with the next exhibit to see what was involved. The board member became one of Pickard's strongest supporters after becoming more intimately familiar with operations. A potential disaster was turned into a wonderful opportunity.

Table 6.8. Case Study 2—Tips

Kelli Pickard's Tips for Improving Board Relations
1. Be forthcoming and transparent. This is particularly important since city management may not understand the operations of the museum.
2. Prepare monthly reports to the city management or governing authority about what you are doing.
3. Communicate frequently. Don't wait for meetings to talk to decision-makers.
4. Find your advocates and ask them to be vocal in their support.
5. Learn the politics of the system and adapt to them.

Case Study 3

My first position as a small museum director was only my second job after I completed a master's degree in museum studies at Texas Tech University. I had been working as a registrar at a large museum in Atlanta and found that I missed interaction with the public. I had always known I wanted to be a small museum director because I am a generalist and wanted to get my hands into everything. I was thrilled to be brought into this small local history museum. But I had no idea what questions to ask or exactly what was expected of me at first. I certainly knew what I thought I should be doing and was somewhat surprised when that did not match the board's expectations.

The museum was a 501(c)(3) private nonprofit founded in 1993 with an annual budget of $150,000. The staff included a director, a full-time archivist, a part-time bookkeeper, and a part-time store manager. The board consisted of twelve individuals, but efforts were under way to grow it to eighteen members. The only giving requirement was an annual membership, costing a minimum of $35. Terms were limited to two years with a second term possible without rotation off the board. The board was not racially or ethnically diverse, though it was gender and age diverse. It was not representative of the community we were serving.

I learned shortly after I started in the position that the bylaws stated that the president of the board was the CEO of the museum. My title was museum director, but I was more of a managing director. It took many months for me to feel my way through these new waters and to understand the boundaries of my authority. Eventually I found a good rhythm with the

Table 6.9. Case Study 3—Key Facts

Institution and Location: Rome Area History Museum, Rome, Georgia
Administrator: Katie Anderson, Museum Director

Type of Governance	Private 501(c)(3)		
Budget	$150,000	**Founded**	1993
Staff Size	2 FT + 2 PT	**Size of Board**	12–18

president, and I learned a great deal from him. Three years into my four-year tenure, he resigned for personal reasons. He had been the president since the museum opened, and transitioning to a new president was challenging. The board member selected to succeed the retiring president had joined the board a few months earlier. She and I had clashed shortly after she joined the board. I knew that she and I would not be strong partners able to effectively move the museum forward. Additionally, there were not enough strong personalities on the board with whom I could form alliances. Therefore, I chose to seek a position with another organization. When I handed in my resignation, I had already found not only a new position at the Rome Area History Museum (RAHM) but also my replacement.

During my tenure at RAHM, I learned by trial and error. I spent most of my energy on marketing, community outreach, exhibits, educational programming, grant writing, completely reworking the gift shop, and automating office processes. I was able to reduce staff and raise awareness and interest in the community. I was fortunate that I had been told I was not responsible for fundraising. At the same time, my opinions and recommendations about fundraising were not always welcomed. For example, when a board member tried to tell people their raffle-ticket purchases were tax deductible, I explained that was incorrect. I was able to get the written statement on the tickets removed, but the communication of this erroneous information continued verbally.

While I was not responsible for fundraising, I knew the only way I could hire an educator was to find the money myself. So I wrote and received a $56,000 two-year Museums for America grant from the Institute of Museum and Library Services (IMLS). This grant would not have been possible without the prior work of the former director, who developed the museum's first multiyear strategic plan. Achieving the first federal grant and being able to put the IMLS logo on our website, front door, and brochure gave the board and me momentum. It raised the bar.

My biggest success related to the board was getting its commitment to complete a Museum Assessment Program for Organizational Assessment (OMAP)

Table 6.10. Case Study 3—Tips

Katie Anderson's Tips for Improving Board Relations
1. Be friendly—greet them with a smile even if you have twenty things you need to be doing.
2. Show a genuine interest in why they support the museum and *listen*.
3. Be enthusiastic and productive. Be excited about your work and share that with them.
4. Communicate. Focus on talking and listening to individual board members as often as possible. Spend more time than you think you have communicating with the board.
5. Being flexible can help you accept it when things don't go your way. It can also help you be open to unexpected opportunities.
6. Learn to delegate and let go! You can't do it all yourself.

through AAM. Getting a board of influential civic leaders to do what equates to a self-evaluation willingly is no small task! This museum had never done anything like this. We had just finished the self-evaluation when I resigned.

Signs That It May Be Time to Leave: Fact or Fable?

Jane always wanted to be a museum director. Throughout her graduate studies, she took diverse courses in museum law, education, exhibitions, collections management, and administration. She loved every aspect and wanted to do all of it! After several years of museum work in various capacities, she became the director of a small local history museum with a staff of four.

The financial-reporting system for the museum was flawed and needed considerable work to provide an accurate and complete picture of the financial situation. Reports were finally ready after many months of implementing a new reporting system while simultaneously opening a new exhibit, dealing with angry and complacent staff who had not had a director for six months, completely changing the store layout and product line, implementing a point-of-sale system in the store, revamping the website, creating an online store, designing and producing a new full-color newsletter, and successfully wooing disgruntled volunteers.

Despite the fact that huge strides had been made in various other areas of the museum, the financial picture was dire. Long-standing prior debt from the purchase of products for the store was settled after several years of stagnation. Though attendance had increased, a national recession meant a decrease in cash donations. The good news was that a buzz about the quality of exhibits and programming had been generated. The black-and-white newsletter was now full color with exquisite photos and articles. People were genuinely excited about where the museum was going. The bad news was that the financial picture seemed to indicate the museum was not sustainable without drastic changes.

Jane was a wreck. She worked six-day weeks trying to do all the marketing to keep people excited and participating, working with the board on fundraising, managing the volunteers and staff, managing the museum and store, and preparing for board meetings. She cared deeply about the museum, the staff, and the community. She made herself sick worrying about her staff's livelihood, the founder's expectations, and the possibility that the museum might close.

During this time she developed a close relationship with the board chair, Linda, whom she greatly respected. Jane began to lean on Linda and confide in her about various problems and Jane's own feelings of inadequacy to handle such a major crisis. Jane was very upfront with the board when she was interviewed. She told them she had very little fundraising experience, and though she was eager to learn, she would need help.

At first Linda and the other board members were patient and supportive. But at one particular board meeting, things turned ugly. Although the financial information had been shared at every board meeting, a change in the way it was presented caused everyone to finally see how serious the situation was. Jane had not understood that the board was not seeing the picture clearly. One board member, Henry, blamed Jane, even though she had inherited the situation.

An unexpected bequest created a small buffer, and the board decided it was time to hire the museum's first development professional. Jane interviewed several candidates who wanted more money than the museum could afford, more in fact than Jane's own salary. It took two months to find a strong candidate. An offer was made and accepted. The new development person worked for one month and left for her dream job. It took another six months to hire a replacement. In the meantime the board became more anxious. Jane tried her best to do the things she knew would build a solid foundation for fundraising. After all, you cannot raise money if no one knows about your organization or everyone thinks it is stagnant.

When Carol was hired, everyone was excited about her experience and enthusiasm. But when the board did not see substantial results in two months, they decided that Carol should report to Henry, who was an experienced fundraiser in the social services arena. Carol was concerned about reporting to a board member, but she tried to work with Henry despite not agreeing with his approach. Henry's background with a large, well-known social services organization was not translating well to a small, unknown cultural organization.

Soon Henry was accusing Jane of being obstructionist and disrespectful to Henry whenever she asked a question. The tension made Jane loathe board meetings. She never felt that she could prepare enough and was expecting angry words at each meeting. The board asked Jane for a recommendation for cutting staffing levels. Linda's term as board chair came to an end at that time, and Henry became the new chair.

When Carol had been at the museum for four months, the board decided she was not going to work out. At that same meeting, Jane presented her plan for staffing reduction. Henry did not agree with any of Jane's ideas.

Around this time, a consultant advised the board members to hold an executive session so that they could freely discuss issues without worrying that they would hurt Jane's feelings or be embarrassed for not knowing as much as she did about what was going on. Jane objected and was told this was common practice for other nonprofits in the area. The only example given was a social service organization, not a museum.

The board decided it needed to conduct a series of emergency strategic-planning meetings to look at the financial situation. Jane was not invited.

While it is the board's role to ensure effective strategic planning for the museum, it cannot do this effectively without the input of the director. Without Jane in the room, the board lost the operational perspective and did not have as clear an understanding of what the consequences would be. As the administrator, Jane had unsurpassable operational knowledge. She was on the front line. She saw how visitors responded to exhibits and programming. She heard what people in the community were saying about the museum. She knew what donors wanted to support and why they were or were not supporting the museum. She knew what her staff could handle and what would not get done if staff was reduced. And she knew what programs and activities were critical to keep the museum relevant.

After the first meeting, Jane was given two options. Option 1 was that she could stay on as the director, stop doing any marketing, spend 75 percent of her time doing fundraising (it had previously been 25 percent), fire the professional fundraiser (Carol), and keep the curator/educator. Option 2 was that she could fire Carol and the curator/educator, become the next curator/educator, and let the board hire a new director/fundraiser.

This had become an untenable situation. Jane could not see herself working for a new director after having been the director for two years. She also knew that she would end up working eighty or more hours per week if she agreed to Option 1 and that there would be no guarantee of success.

Jane knew that in the short term this concentrated focus on fundraising to the exclusion of programming could work to stop the financial crisis. But without exciting exhibits and programming and the marketing to promote them, she felt strongly that eventually supporters would lose interest. This is why marketing falls under the direction of the development department in many larger museums. They go hand in hand. A strong public relations program is critical to fundraising, especially if you are a little-known special-interest museum struggling for community awareness. Because of that, Jane knew she would need to continue doing marketing and public relations while adding more fundraising duties to her plate, meaning her sixty-hour weeks would increase to approximately seventy-five- to eighty-hour workweeks for the foreseeable future. Jane was not interested in that prospect.

It was a difficult situation for everyone. The board needed to make hard decisions to uphold its fiduciary responsibilities. The money to pay staff and utilities was simply not coming in. But Jane also knew that cutting programming, exhibits, and marketing would mean that people would lose interest in the museum. Feeling that she could not possibly meet the current needs of the museum without serious consequences to her health and peace of mind and that within six months she would likely be terminated, Jane resigned with no job prospects on the horizon.

What key factors told Jane that the board's loss of confidence in her was irreversible?

- The board was conducting strategic planning meetings without her.
- The board insisted on having a staff person report to it directly.
- Her job description changed dramatically, including a potential demotion.
- The new board chair did not agree with her on most topics.
- Communication and trust continued to erode.

Maybe you recognize your own situation here and there in the preceding fable. What decision would you have made in Jane's shoes?

While the story conflates my experiences at various museums, as well as stories I have heard from others, each of the five bullet points has happened to me and eventually led to my leaving a position. Several happened simultaneously. Any one of them can make it nearly impossible to move forward as a director and as an organization.

Through hard work, determination, and staff changes, I had succeeded in raising the level of professionalism in the two museums I administered over a seven-year period. The founders wanted to work toward accreditation. I was making progress in that direction. In both cases, the boards' direction for the museums changed, and I chose not to change with it. This happens. It is best to be able to see this as it is happening and respond on your own terms. Every director brings something different to the museum. While each may be competent and valued, none will not be the perfect fit for every stage of a museum's existence. Know when it is your time, and leave gracefully and professionally.

Conclusion

Every relationship between a board and director of a small museum is unique. Like any important relationship, this complex partnership needs sustained and vigilant attention and nurturing. This is a partnership between a single individual and multiple people, all with different perspectives and motivations. Taking the time to get to know each board member can pay great dividends. You will undoubtedly be more comfortable with some than others. So embrace the differences and move ahead.

Ask for clear guidance about what the board sees as the boundaries of your authority. It is important to understand this to avoid serious clashes. You need to be able to act with confidence. Knowing the boundaries will help.

Open communication between the board and the director is critical. The board needs to communicate any of its concerns frankly to the director. Evaluating the director's performance is one of the main roles of the board. I feel strongly that the board should meet without the director only when it is explicitly and systematically evaluating her or his performance.

Take every opportunity to educate board members on museum operations and standards. The more they understand, the less resistance you may meet. This task takes tremendous energy and can seem thankless and neverending, but it is absolutely necessary.

The final word on director-board relations is communication. You must spend more time than you think is necessary or than you think you can afford talking to and listening to your board members. They can be your biggest fans or your biggest detractors. How well and how often you communicate with them sets the stage for your success and the success of your museum. Ups and downs will occur in any relationship between a director and his or her governing board. Ideally, you will enjoy the ups and learn from the downs. In my experience, the downs, much more so than the ups, have provided invaluable insights into my own character and lessons that will benefit me for a lifetime. Each director contributes something different to a museum. If you can look back and say your tenure helped build the foundation for future directors, you have accomplished a great deal.

Resources

American Association for State and Local History. *Standards and Excellence Program for History Organizations Workbook.* Nashville, TN: AASLH, 2009.

Andringa, Robert C., and Ted W. Engstrom. *Nonprofit Board Answer Book: Practical Guide for Board Members and Chief Executives.* Washington, DC: BoardSource, 2002.

Bradt, George, Jayme A. Check, and Jorge Pedraza. *The New Leader's 100-Day Action Plan: How to Take Charge, Build Your Team, and Get Immediate Results.* 3rd ed. Hoboken, NJ: John Wiley & Sons, 2011.

Carver, John. *The Carver Guide Series on Effective Board Governance.* San Francisco: Jossey-Bass.

Cohen, Dan S. *The Heart of Change Field Guide: Tools and Tactics for Leading Change in Your Organization.* Boston: Harvard Business School Press, 2005.

Knowledge@Wharton: http://knowledge.wharton.upenn.edu.

Small Museums Yahoo! Group Listserv: http://groups.yahoo.com/group/SmallMuseums/.

INDEX

ABOUT THE EDITORS

Cinnamon Catlin-Legutko has worked in the small museum world since 1994 and was the director of the General Lew Wallace Study & Museum in Crawfordsville, Indiana, from 2003 to 2009. In 2008, the museum was awarded the National Medal for Museum Service. Her contributions to the field include leadership of the AASLH Small Museums Committee, service as an IMLS grant reviewer and AAM MAP peer reviewer, and service as an AASLH Council member. She is now CEO of the Abbe Museum in Bar Harbor, Maine.

Stacy Klingler currently serves local history organizations as the assistant director of local history services at the Indiana Historical Society. She began her career in museums as the assistant director of two small museums, before becoming director of the Putnam County Museum in Greencastle, Indiana. She chairs the AASLH's Small Museums Committee (2008–2012) and attended the Seminar for Historical Administration in 2006. While she lives in the history field, her passion is encouraging a love of learning in any environment.

ABOUT THE CONTRIBUTORS

Cherie Cook is senior program manager for the American Association for State and Local History (AASLH). Prior to joining AASLH in 2005, Cook served as executive director of the Oklahoma Museums Association (1993–2004), Oklahoma field advisory service coordinator (1988–1993), and curator of the Reno County (Kansas) Historical Society (1985–1988). She holds a master's in historical administration from Eastern Illinois University and a bachelor's in history from Kansas State University.

Elizabeth Merritt is the founding director of the Center for the Future of Museums, a think tank and research-and-development lab for the museum field. The American Association of Museums (AAM) created the center to help museums explore cultural, political, and economic trends shaping the future and ensure that museums play a profound role in society. Merritt has over fifteen years of experience in museums, including administration, curation, and collections management. Before joining the AAM in 1999, she was director of collections and research at Cincinnati Museum Center. Her books include *National Standards and Best Practices for U.S. Museums* and the *AAM Guide to Collections Planning*.

Sara Gonzales is coordinator of the Conservation Assessment Program (CAP) at Heritage Preservation. A graduate of the Museum Studies Program at the University of Wisconsin, Milwaukee, she has been the collections manager of a number of small museums in the suburbs of Chicago. Her previous publications include issues of *CAPabilities*, CAP's biannual newsletter, and articles about CAP in the AAM's *Museum* and the AASLH's *History News* magazines.

Steve Friesen is director of the Buffalo Bill Museum and Grave near Denver, Colorado. He has worked in small museums since beginning his career in 1976 and, for twenty-seven of those years, has served as administrator for small museums in Kansas, Colorado, and Pennsylvania. Friesen has a master's in American folk culture and is the author of two books, *A Modest Mennonite Home* and *Buffalo Bill: Scout, Showman, Visionary.*

Harold Skramstad and **Susan Skramstad** are internationally recognized museum planning consultants. Harold Skramstad served for over fifteen years as president of the Henry Ford Museum & Greenfield Village. Prior to that, he served as director of the Chicago Historical Society and in several senior administrative posts at the Smithsonian Institution's National Museum of American History. Susan Skramstad served as the vice chancellor for institutional advancement at the University of Michigan, Dearborn. They have served a wide variety of clients both in the United States and abroad in the planning of new museums as well as providing strategic, interpretive, and fundraising planning services to existing museums.

Their work has been recognized at the highest levels. In 1992 Harold Skramstad received the Charles Frankel Prize (now renamed the National Humanities Medal) from President George H. W. Bush for his achievement in bringing the humanities to a broad public audience. In 1994 President William Jefferson Clinton appointed him to the National Council on the Humanities. During his term on the council, he served as chairman of the Public Programs Committee. In 2002 President George W. Bush appointed him to the presidential commission to establish an action plan for a new National Museum of African American History and Culture.

Teresa Goforth holds a master's in history from Michigan State University. She teaches museum studies at Michigan State University and Central Michigan University and is an exhibit developer for the consulting firm Museum Explorer, Inc. Formerly the director of a small museum, she was also part, for five years, of the Museum on Main Street team, a joint project between the Smithsonian Institution Traveling Exhibition Service and the Federation of State Humanities Councils.

Katie Anderson has worked in museums of various sizes for over twelve years and is currently head of registration and collections management at the Musical Instrument Museum in Phoenix, Arizona. For seven years, she was the director of two small museums in Georgia and Arizona. Anderson was an active member of the board of AAM's Small Museum Administrator's Committee and in 2009 served as its program chair.

23501266R00100

Printed in Great Britain
by Amazon